REVIEWS

"*Voices of Courage* has done exactly what it was meant to do: given a 'voice' to survivors of sexual trauma. For survivors of sexual assault, healing is a 'process,' the first step of which is finding a voice. *Voices of Courage* has put words where there previously were none and done it with real women and men, with real stories to tell."

— *Beth-Anne Blue, PhD.*
Psychologist, University of Florida

"*Voices of Courage* gives voice to the phenomenal courage of male and female survivors of sexual violence. Their telling of what was done to them is a wake up call to the brutality of perpetrators and depth of the trauma caused when sex is used as a weapon. But the gift of this book is so much more; it is the healing that comes from not keeping the perpetrators secret, and the power in knowing no one can take away your worth or ability to help others."

— *Cordelia Anderson*
Prevention Consultant, Trainer, & Speaker with Sensibilities, Inc.

"A wonderful collection of diverse victims stories, told crisply and directly, and each with a different message. Many voices speaking through poetry, journals, and stark description of terrible experiences . . . but more important, recovery from them. In these terrible experiences, honestly told, lies a hidden grace—that of coming to new understandings and finding directions for recovery."

— *Gary R. Schoener*
Psychologist, Author, & Expert on Sexual Violence by Professionals

"I have read many texts written both by scholars and by the victims of sexual violence attempting to understand this horrible event from a socio-scientific perspective. What those accounts tend to lack, and what this book does beautifully, is to simply and honestly convey real men and women of all ages telling real stories. The effect is not only humbling, but offers a rarely seen side of rape and sexual assault: The human side. The body of literature on the subject of sexual assault is significantly improved by the publication of this noble volume."

— *Dr. Joseph D. Diaz*
Associate Professor of Sociology
& Director of the Survey Research Center
Fayetteville State University, North Carolina

REVIEWS

"If you have never heard anyone speak about the lingering torment of rape, you will be rudely awakened by the personal stories in *Voices of Courage*. If you are a survivor and have never spoken to anyone, this may give you the courage to begin to deal with the pain it has caused, and give you some great suggestions for healing."

— *Rob Rephan*
  Education and Prevention Specialist, Alliance Against
  Family Violence & Sexual Assault

"These are the articulate, powerful voices of survivors among us, those who have found justice and healing in the midst of trauma. From a woman pastor to a woman victimized by her male pastor, these stories, which are not atypical, present our faith communities with a strong challenge to open our eyes and find new ways to help make justice real in people's lives."

— *Rev. Dr. Marie M. Fortune*
  Founder of FaithTrust Institute and author of
  Sexual Violence: the Sin Revisited

"This book is unique in that it focuses on the ultimate outcome that sexual assault can have on survivors—finding strength and knowledge that may never have been discovered or realized had the experience not occurred. While doing that, the stories still manage to avoid minimizing the challenges implicit in healing from such an experience, which is an impressive balance to find. The book would be very helpful for those exploring how they can use their own experience of trauma to end violence in our society."

— *Serena Clardie, MSW, LCSW*
  Aurora Sexual Assault Treatment Center

"*Voices Of Courage* increases awareness of the complex issue of sexual assault. It opens the eyes of everyone trying to understand the problem, solve the problem, or support a loved one who has been victimized. Most importantly, the book will help many to make the transition from victim to survivor status."

— *Catherine Bath*
  Executive Director, Security On Campus, Inc.

VOICES OF COURAGE

VOICES OF COURAGE

Inspiration from Survivors of Sexual Assault

Edited by Michael J. Domitrz

AWARENESS
PUBLICATIONS
Greenfield, Wisconsin

Copyediting by Joan Ruffino
Cover and text design by Georgene Schreiner

2009   08   07   06   05   5   4   3   2   1

Printed in the United States of America
First Edition 2005

ISBN: 0-9729282-1-9
Library of Congress Control Number: 2005900684

Publisher's Cataloging-in-Publication Data

Domitrz, Michael J.
  Voices of courage: inspiration from survivors of sexual assault/[compiled by] Michael J. Domitrz.—1st ed.—Greenfield, Wis. : Awareness Publications, c2005.
  p. ; cm.
  ISBN: 0-9729282-1-9
  1. Sexual abuse victims' writings. 2. Rape—Social aspects.
3. Sex crimes—Social aspects. 4. Rape—Psychological aspects.
5. Sex crimes—Psychological aspects. 6. Rape victims—Mental health.
7. Sexual abuse victims—Mental health. 8. Post-traumatic stress disorder—Prevention.
I. Domitrz, Michael J.

HV6556 .V65 2005   2005900684
362.883—dc22   0504

Production Assistance by Printstar Publishing, LLC
www.ppub.com

Published by

**AWARENESS
PUBLICATIONS**

P.O. Box 20906, Greenfield WI 53220-0906
800-329-9650 www.awarenesspublications.com

This book is dedicated to all survivors of sexual assault. We are humbled by your strength and courage. You are our inspiration.

With Special Thanks

To the twelve incredible survivors who have shared their lives in order to make this book a reality, thank you! In gifting us your thoughts and emotions, and sharing your pain and triumphs, you have helped others discover the courageous voice of sexual assault survivors.

To the many individuals and organizations dedicated to raising awareness and educating the public, thank you for your ceaseless efforts to open the minds and hearts of the world.

To the dedicated professionals who assist in the healing process, thank you for your your compassion and understanding and your commitment to making a difference in the lives of survivors.

To the loving families and friends of sexual assault survivors, thank you for your strength and support in the journey toward healing and survival.

To the dynamic team at Printstar, Nick Laird, Georgene Schreiner, Joan Ruffino, and Susan Pittelman, thank you for sharing your talent to help create *Voices of Courage*.

VOICES OF COURAGE

CONTENTS

PREFACE

Optimism, courage, and hope are not words you would typically associate with the tragedy of rape and sexual assault. The first emotion most people think of is fear. Have you ever faced fear—the kind of overwhelming fear you can't convey to someone unless they have experienced it themselves? The twelve individuals in this book have experienced that fear and found the courage to face it. They share the wisdom they have gained from living with tragedy and then moving forward to rebuild productive lives. They demonstrate how to use the fire burning inside you to fill your life and the lives of many others with hope and optimism.

What makes this book different from other stories of survival? The diversity of experiences and the striking parallels in the voices of these survivors. Typically, when a person survives a tragedy, society is eager to talk about the perils the person overcame. One exception exists: the tragedy of sexual assault. Instead of being admired, the survivors of sexual assault are all too frequently shunned or even blamed for the horrific actions of the perpetrator. In those cases where the survivors are believed, they are often treated with pity, not respect. No admiration is given for all the pain and trauma they have endured and survived. Their voices are rarely given a chance to be heard.

Many years ago, one survivor did share her "voice" with me and changed my life forever. She was my sister. When she was raped in 1989, I knew our lives would never be the same. I questioned what I could believe in. I thought to myself, "I am not even the victim; how is my sister ever going to move forward?" She did far more than move forward. She went on to become my role model, a model of strength and courage. Her determination inspired me to dedicate my life to speaking in schools and on college campuses about the many societal issues surrounding sexual assault.

At the end of each of my speeches, at least one person in the audience would invariably approach me. The look on his or her face would be one of great concern—like a person about to tell you some really bad news. The person would ask, "How is your sister doing?" I could tell that he or she assumed that all the happiness in my sister's life was over. I would then explain how magnificently my sister was doing in each aspect of her life. The audience member was always surprised and suddenly relieved. Having been asked this question so many times, it seems most people naturally assume my sister must be doing poorly; but why? The answer is clear; our society does not highlight success stories from the survivors of sexual assault. Survivors are invited to talk only about "how" they were assaulted and are rarely given a voice to discuss their recovery and how great their lives are today.

As you read this book, you will hear the voices of twelve amazing survivors—their own stories in their own words. Each chapter has been written by a different survivor. You will experience their anger, strength, compassion, joy, and their love. You will be moved by their emotion and enlightened by the truth they speak. They will share their insights, their struggles, how they succeeded, and how they are doing today. As you finish each chapter, you will be uplifted and inspired by the strength and courage these role models display on a daily basis.

You will likely notice that the experiences, emotions, and reactions of these survivors remind you of people you know and love. That should come as no surprise; this crime is perpetrated against people of all backgrounds regardless of age, race, gender, sexual orientation, marital status, physical capabilities, culture, upbringing, or location. Their stories may even remind you of you. If you are a survivor of sexual assault, *Voices of Courage* has been written to provide you with opportunities to connect with the personal experiences of other survivors. If at anytime you feel a need to communicate with someone, a list of resources is provided at the back of the book. Please do not hesitate to call one of the 24-hour toll-free numbers provided or to send an e-mail to one of the many online resources.

Voices of Courage is filled with powerful lessons and countless examples of courage and personal discovery. Whether married or single, teenager or adult, you are about to learn powerful lessons about health and happiness from twelve inspiring people, who are all survivors of sexual assault.

Michael Domitrz

Voices of Courage was produced to provide inspiration, heighten awareness, reduce sexual assault, and to aid survivors. All profits from the sale of this book are being given to organizations that address issues surrounding sexual assault.

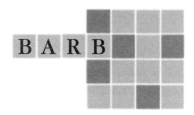

BARB

"There's going to be nothing left . . . nothing left. . . . Oh my God, there's going to be nothing left." I must have said that to myself a hundred times as he was raping me on the cement basement floor. "There's going to be nothing left . . . nothing left . . . nothing left of me."

There was plenty left. Of course, you couldn't have convinced me of that at the time. I felt totally void, as cold as that cement floor. But I was not destroyed by this experience. Instead, I am stronger than I was before. After my rape, I played over and over again a favorite song that gave me strength. One line in the song resonated for me: "Spirit is something no one destroys." I fell back on those words all the time; still do. It is a belief that has held up through talking with other survivors of sexual assault for the past eighteen years.

Often, I am asked how I can work as an advocate for women who have been sexually victimized. "Don't I find it depressing and sad?" I reply no. I am inspired by the resiliency of the human spirit. We are women who have endured one of the most degrading acts that can be perpetrated against us. Even worse, these acts are usually committed by our boyfriends, husbands, male family members, male friends, or acquaintances. Yet, here we stand, our spirits intact.

Being raped by a stranger is horrific, but when we are raped by someone we know, someone we trust, someone whom we thought knew and respected us, we face an overwhelming sense of betrayal. It is highly personalized. Self-blame runs deep. I've learned through my own experience and from listening to other women that self-blame is usually the last thing we give up. While it may sound odd, I've come to realize that remorse is a coping mechanism. As long as I felt I was to blame for being raped, I felt I had control over what had happened to me. Believing that I may have had some role in the assault gave me an illusion of power at a time when I felt I had none. The hardest thing for me to do was to admit, "No matter what I did, no matter what I said, no matter how hard I tried, I couldn't stop him from doing what he did to me. I couldn't stop him from saying what he said to me. I couldn't stop him. I was powerless." That was humiliating for me.

But more difficult was the point in the healing process when I was ready to admit that I was not to blame. That was very frightening. At that moment, I was truly stripped of my sense of power, even though that sense had been only an illusion all along. Suddenly, I was faced with my own vulnerability; there was no way to deny that the same man or some other man could do this to me again.

Talking with other survivors has taught me that while we aren't totally destroyed by this violence committed against us, we are forever altered. We will never look at the world the same way. We will never be the people we were before. For an entire year, I was tormented by the idea that I had to get everything back to the way it had been before. It took me a long time to accept the fact that this was an impossibility, that I must grieve the loss of my previous self.

I am convinced that my sense of powerlessness over what had been done to me set the stage for my eating disorder of anorexia nervosa. It makes perfect sense that eating disorders occur in survivors. Invariably, we feel that our right to control what happens to our bodies has been taken from us. What better way to regain a sense of control over our physical selves than to rigidly restrict what we eat? I often find myself getting exasperated with anorexia "experts" who focus only on issues of body image and self esteem. I wasn't concerned merely with how I looked or how I felt about myself. For me, the disorder was about reclaiming control over my own body.

But there was a price to pay. After the rape, I felt an indescribable sense of unworthiness and ultimately, anorexia was a form of self-inflicted punishment for being such an awful person. My thought process at the time was that food was healthy; food was good for me. But I believed I was not worthy of anything good and I certainly didn't want to nourish my violated body. Anorexia allowed me to prove to myself that I could decide how my body would be treated, even if that meant punishing it. But while I may have reclaimed decision-making power over my own body, I was slowly committing suicide; I wanted to die.

A teenager I was working with after she had been assaulted summed it up best. This young woman, who had been raped about a year earlier, was taking risks with her health by being promiscuous.

I recognized that in addition to being a normal reaction to assault, promiscuity is often caused by poor self esteem, and I attempted to address that problem as I had been trained to do. I was going by the book and she became exasperated with me. She looked at me with her hair hanging down in her face and sneered, "You just don't get it, do you? It's just easier being a thing." Now, that I could get. She was right. It is easier to be a thing than to take on human emotions and feel intense pain. To face that depth of despair is to enter a deep, dark, frightening chasm. But it's worth it, for when we emerge, it is into a place of light and calm. The result of surviving that dark place is an amazing strength.

Although we are made stronger, we often have a hard time maintaining the interpersonal relationships we had prior to the rape; if we aren't the same, then how can we fit into the same relationships? Often, despite the incredible support we may have from a significant other, we end up severing ties to that person. By the same token, the changes that occur during the aftermath of an assault also explain why significant others may withdraw from us. I often hear, "I just want her to be like she was before." I hate to be the one to break the bad news, but that's not going to happen. That certainly doesn't mean that as survivors, we won't rebuild and heal; it simply means that "healed" is not the same as "restored."

People seem to be more understanding about other kinds of tragedies. My sister was twenty-three when she died. I was twenty-two. It was a beautiful September day when I got the phone call that she had been in a car accident. The doctors tried to stabilize her for surgery but were unable to do so. The next day, she was unhooked from life support and died. I am not the same person I was before experiencing her death; I am not able to look at the world the same way. I was immediately and forever changed by the loss of my sister, and people understood and accepted this. No one expected that I would go on as if nothing had happened. No one expected me to be "normal." No one expected me to be in class the next day and to keep up with my academic work. My friends knew that I would have days when I was overwhelmed with pain and angst. My family expected that I would have nightmares. It was okay that I would need to speak of that experience again and again. No one expected me to "just get over it;" they understood that it was only natural that I go through the grieving process. Why should the process of grieving the loss of the girl or woman you were before the rape be any different?

I want to give survivors, including myself, permission to feel whatever it is we are feeling. I want to empower the significant others in our lives with insights that will help the women in their lives. While I understand that our feelings and reactions can be frustrating, even downright exasperating, perhaps when our loved ones better understand us, we will be able to grow and heal.

Our friends, family members, and significant others aren't the only people who can benefit from learning to be patient during our healing process. Service providers, especially within the criminal justice system, need to have patience. As an advocate of survivors, all too often I hear from police officers, detectives and prosecutors that they are unwilling to further investigate or to file charges in sexual assault cases due in part to the victim's initial response to the assault. This may include a delay in reporting the assault, removing or cleaning physical evidence, an inability to recall quickly and clearly the events that took place, and withholding information about the assault. These reactions are completely normal, yet I'm afraid to recall the number of times I've heard criminal justice personnel say with a shrug that because of these reactions, there is nothing they can do. We need to be more creative in how we investigate and prosecute these cases. We cannot simply throw up our hands in exasperation. Author John Brunner wrote, "If there is such a phenomenon as absolute evil, it consists in treating another human being as a thing." Survivors face this kind of evil when they are sexually assaulted. We often face it again from investigators, prosecutors, and others who may consider us "cases" rather than people. We deserve more respect as we face the aftermath of sexual assault. The normal reactions of survivors are not going to change. Therefore, we as a society must change our response to these reactions.

As a survivor of many years, I feel whole and healthy. I have for a long time. I think a lot of that has come from my speaking out, but more importantly from listening to the wisdom of survivors. While I still work in the field of advocacy for survivors of sexual assault, and while I feel a great sense of support in doing so, it is not my own experience that compels me to do this work. What drives me is a strong sense of justice. I am affronted by the attitudes in our culture that condone these acts. I am offended that these acts even occur. I am outraged that little or nothing is done to hold many rapists accountable. It all stems from women not being equally valued in our society. Until we are fully valued for who we uniquely are, not for how we compare to men, women will continue to be subjected to humiliation and degradation in every aspect of our culture. Until society fully values women, we will continue to have men who rape, a justice system that does not respond adequately, and women who are treated as "things." The current state of affairs is simply unjust. Something needs to be done and I vow to be one of the many working to end the violence.

SHIRLEY

Allow for the Possibility

Was there a time when I didn't feel left out?

I don't think so.

I didn't belong. I didn't fit in.

I was different from the other kids.

I even ate differently!

Cereal—no milk.

French fries—no ketchup.

Hamburgers—plain.

Food had to be dry.

Raw potatoes enticed me.

"No one's looking!" Grab one—sneak it to the bedroom,

take a few bites and hide it in the closet.

I couldn't eat school lunches.

A teacher forced me to drink milk once.

I threw up on her shoes.

VOICES OF COURAGE

Six years of peanut butter sandwiches,
no jelly and no butter—food had to be dry.
My bed was a different story—it was wet.

I wet the bed for years.
The doctor stretched my urethra,
but urine stained my sheets
and tears wet my pillow.
Was I the only one who felt this way?
Was I the only one?

Middle child with no special place.
My brother was firstborn and a boy.
My sister, the first daughter.
Then came me.
My other sister, the baby.
Each had a special place.
But not me, stuck in the middle.
That was why, they said, I always felt so bad.
No one knew the truth.

The neighbors all thought Daddy was great.
They didn't know he liked to hurt little girls.

I greeted junior high, my closest friends at my side:
Shame, Depression and Anger.
They went everywhere with me.

Could no one see them?
I learned to cover them up.

Already an expert at secrets,
I wrote suicide notes.
Begging to be rescued.
I took long walks in the country and wrote poetry.
Sometimes I exploded and took off—Running.
Mamma worried. I know she did.
So I always came home.

There were two teachers.
One in Junior High and one in High School.
We connected.
They saw my talents and potential.
They saw value in me.
They ignited the spark of hope that visited now and then
when my friends weren't around.
Two teachers.
I am grateful to them.

My invisible friends grew bigger and darker.
I couldn't get away from them.
"Why doesn't somebody help me?" I wept.
I hated myself, my life.

Out of school and out of the house.
Finally, I was free.

VOICES OF COURAGE

As I searched for happiness,
those monsters traveled with me.
Shame, Depression and Anger.
Deep inside I knew something was wrong.
What?

No memories before sixth grade.
Not one.
Had there been a trauma . . . ?
Childhood memories buried.
In order to survive?

I couldn't trust people,
I didn't trust myself.
Relationships were superficial,
fleeting.

School and work defined me.
I became a perfectionist
in order to feel better about myself.
To the world, I was strong and competent.
Inside, I was a mess.

There were gifts:
Working with exceptional people.
Lessons in openness,
in love and grace.

There were clues:
Passion for people with disabilities,
Compassion for those who had been abused.
Reverence for those who endured,
Honor in bravery.

I was a suicidal person
until I became a mother.
I struggled,
but suicide was no longer an option for me.
Mothers don't do that to their children, I told myself.
But the pain continued.

Forty-three: a great professional life!
Personally?
Divorced, single parent, bad relationship.
I was miserable.
One night I found myself in a twelve-step program.
The healing began
. . . I chose healing.

In those first few months,
I learned coping skills
that prepared me.
For coming crises.

Forty-four: I discovered where my childhood went.
I discovered that my father is a pedophile.

Beyond difficult.
But supportive people were in my life.
Gone were Shame, Depression and Anger.

Everything I needed to recover had been put in my path.
I was told,
"You are only as sick as your secrets."
And out they poured.

A turning point:
I gave up the hope of a different childhood.
Why do we hold on to such things?

I have discovered what nourishes me.
I have learned to
release that which does not serve my highest good.
I have learned that
I can be open and honest
and still be loved.

In places, my childhood has returned
and I am unashamed.

It has not been an easy journey.
Those old friends—you remember them—try to seduce me back
every now and then.

I remind myself that recovery has layers
and that when the pain returns,
I can embrace it,
release it,
and move on.

Tears that aren't shed
return to the soul and remain.
Today I release those tears.
I get lighter all the time.

I know my purpose—
sexual abuse prevention and recovery
for those with developmental disabilities.
The doors just keep opening.
I allow for the possibility of a new beginning
every day.
If we hold the suffering of yesterday in one hand
and the worries about tomorrow in the other,
we have no hands for today.

Fifty-two: My life is a joy.
My relationships are real.
I embrace this moment and this day.
Oh, I should mention . . .
I take ketchup with my fries now.

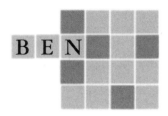

B E N

February 28, 1998 is a day that will stick with me for the rest of my life. It is the day that I was raped. It happened at an off-campus party during my freshman year of college. I don't remember much of that evening other than arriving and having a few drinks. My next memory is waking up on the floor of my dorm shower, crying silently. But this isn't about my rape; it's about what I did afterwards.

I found it difficult to talk with anyone about what had happened, partially because I didn't know what had happened, and also because I didn't know whom I could trust. I didn't know if anyone would believe me. After all, I didn't remember much of what had happened and I had never heard of a guy getting raped. Despite these doubts, I talked with a college counselor the next day. She was helpful and told me that I wasn't alone. She suggested that I go to the hospital and have a rape exam done; she even drove me there since I didn't have a car. Because it had been about sixteen hours since the rape and because I had showered, she suggested I also bring my clothes to be tested. I got a blood test and a rape kit done. I don't remember the rape exam very well, but I remember that the nurse was very empathetic. I later found out that she was a SANE nurse—a sexual assault nurse examiner—who had received specific training on collecting evidence of sexual assault crimes and working with survivors of sexual assault. They didn't find any traces of DNA, but they did find in my blood traces of rohypnol and gamma hydroxyl butyrate (GHB), two drugs known to dampen sensation and negatively affect a person's memory. These drugs are commonly referred to as "predatory drugs."

My counselor suggested that I file a report with the police department. She acknowledged that the likelihood of finding out who raped me was small, but at least it would be documented. I wasn't sure how helpful this would be, but I figured that I might as well do it. Unfortunately, the police were less sympathetic than the nurse and my counselor had been. They didn't take my case very seriously. The hardest part was when the officer who interviewed me didn't believe my story because, he said, guys don't get raped. Even with the presence of predatory drugs in my blood, he thought that I simply felt guilty about trying anal sex with another guy.

Besides my counselor, whom I saw once or twice a month, I didn't really have anyone to confide in. Our campus didn't have a strong sexual assault advocacy group, and the few people who were part of it did not seem very approachable or friendly. I had seen them at a rally and it seemed they believed that "men cause rape." I didn't think they would agree with me that men must be an integral part of the solution against sexual assault. I relied primarily on the Internet, finding online support groups for male survivors. I also found contact information for RAINN—the Rape, Incest & Abuse National Network.

I kept that number in my wallet but didn't call them for several months. Instead, I ignored all of the emotions that I was feeling and pushed ahead with my schoolwork.

It wasn't until I was home that summer that I called the hotline. I was having nightmares and hadn't slept well in a couple of weeks. It was affecting my job and my social life, and friends were beginning to worry about me. My parents were beginning to wonder what was wrong, and despite our close connection, I couldn't bring myself to tell them. I didn't know how they would take the news that their son had been raped and I didn't want to put any emotional stress on them. Late one Friday night, I called RAINN, and they put me in contact with a trained counselor who dealt with a lot of male sexual assaults. That night, I talked for three hours about what had happened. I listened to the counselor as she told me about others who had endured similar situations. That's when I knew that I wasn't alone, that there really were other guys who had been raped.

Over the years, I have talked with many survivors, both men and women, and have found that the road to recovery varies a great deal. Some survivors see counselors, while others are able to continue their lives with relative ease. Many have lingering fears; they might panic if they encounter someone who looks, sounds, or smells like their attacker. I took to writing, something I had done in the past but without the sense of purpose that drives me now. In my writing, I examine my emotions and moods and try to make sense of what has happened to me. I have written poetry and shared it with classmates.

I have done readings at sexual assault awareness events. But the biggest part of the healing process for me has been sharing my experience with others and raising awareness about the inhumanity of sexual assault.

Two years after my rape, I transferred to a different college and met one of the most inspirational people of my life—my peer education advisor. I started working with a peer education group to educate people about alcohol and other drugs. I joined this program because I wanted to promote responsible drinking and spread the message about the potential consequences of drug use. For one journal assignment, we were asked us to write about sexual assault and how we felt about the terms "rape," "sexual assault," "victim," and "survivor." I wrote about my experience. I said I didn't know whether I felt like a victim or a survivor because I didn't know if I had fully dealt with the trauma and my emotions. My advisor called me into his office and thanked me. He told me that he knew I had the potential to change peoples' lives. I still didn't feel that I could. It's one thing to write in a personal journal about your experience. It's another thing altogether to become an agent for change in a violent and unsympathetic world. But he convinced me to take the next step and become an advocate for change.

That summer, I had the opportunity to voice my story. Three friends, my advisor, and I were performing skits about alcohol use, safe sex, and sexual assault for the girls at my former high school. One of the scripts that we performed involved a male survivor of sexual assault. We had chosen it because there was only one woman in the show and we didn't want her to always play the victim role. After the skit, one girl said that she didn't believe the script because guys couldn't get raped. Her misconception was that guys always wanted sex with a girl and that gay guys always wanted sex. I was in the audience at the time and one of my friends looked over at me. He saw that I was affected by this statement. I calmly walked up to the front of the auditorium, grabbed the microphone, and sat down on the edge of the stage. I told them that guys could be raped, by both men and women. I told them that rape wasn't just a women's issue because it affects both men and women. I told them that I was a survivor of sexual assault and I told them my story.

After the performance, I hung around for a bit to answer individual questions and to visit with some of the students who had been freshmen when I graduated. One of the students that I didn't know, a sophomore, handed me a tightly folded piece of paper and asked me to read it later. Several students thanked me and so did some of the teachers. On the car ride back, I opened the note and read it. The girl had written about her own ongoing experience with sexual assault. She explained that her cousin had been raping her for the past year and that her parents didn't believe her. She didn't feel she could go to the police or to her teachers. That night, I called and listened to her as she cried and yelled and vented all of the anger that she had inside. I told her that she wasn't alone and that she was strong for having the courage to tell someone, a complete stranger. I told her about RAINN and that she could get help. Finally, I told her the truth—that being a survivor wasn't easy, that the pain wouldn't just go away one day. At the same time, I told her, being a survivor wasn't a curse that doomed her to a horrible, messed up adult life.

Since then, I have heard stories of many men's and women's experiences with sexual assault. Unfortunately, all too many of the stories that I have heard come from friends and loved ones. I was a resident assistant for two years and sexual assault was the topic of one of our staff meetings. Our hall director asked us to raise our hands if we were comfortable enough to tell the other twenty people in the room that we were survivors of sexual harassment or assault. Thirteen of us raised our hands, including five males. I am no longer surprised to find how prevalent sexual assault is. I have been awakened at 4:00 a.m. because a resident in my building has been forced to have sex with someone, often his or her own boyfriend or girlfriend. I am humbled when people who have just gone through a sexual assault find the courage to trust and confide in me.

As I write this, I am approaching the seven-year anniversary of my rape. Every day, I continue to use my experience to benefit others. I am working on my master's degree in community health, with the goal of working on college campuses to promote health and safety issues that affect young adults. I've often reflected on how I have changed since my rape and, like most survivors, I have wondered how my life would be if I hadn't been raped. As odd as it sounds, I don't think that I would give up my experience for anything in the world. Yes, I think it stinks that I was raped. But because of my experience and the people who have helped me through it, I have been able to turn the rape into a motivation to help others. At the same time, telling people that I am a survivor of sexual assault hasn't gotten easier. It took me about three years to tell my parents and my brother, and I still haven't told some of my closest friends. When I stand up in front of a group of students and talk about sexual assault, I still get butterflies in my stomach, because part of me doesn't want to relive the experience. When I talk with students about sexual assault, I tell them that men can be sexually assaulted and that if they hadn't ever known a male survivor, they do now.

CAROLINE

About two and a half years ago, you forced sex on me after what had begun as a fun and innocent evening. You probably think that what you did was "casual," no big deal, just a logical ending to a great date. But what you did was hurtful and harmful both physically and emotionally. I am still dealing with the consequences of your actions.

For a year, I tried to laugh it off and make a joke about it, to convince myself that what happened was just a mistake I made. My own big mistake. I felt as if I had broken a promise to myself that I would wait for sex until I could share it with the man I loved and married. I blamed myself for what happened. As time passed, the memories were slowly suppressed and so was the truth. I kept it to myself, afraid that people would think less of me if they knew. I felt I had to be the fun, carefree, smiley person I had been before, but something was different. I missed my old self.

Nearly a year later, as I was driving back from spring break, a friend and I were discussing STDs. I had never been checked out and I began to think that I probably should be. Surprisingly, that thought had never crossed my mind. As we rode on, we drove past the city limit sign for your hometown. It didn't register at first, but then it clicked. That was where you were from. The timing was too precise to be coincidental. As insignificant as it seemed, that little road sign triggered memories. For the last eighty miles of the drive, I started to take an honest look at that night. I began to admit that what had happened was not consensual sex. I felt sick to my stomach. It had been bad enough to recall that night as a "mistake." To face the notion that it was rape was a million times worse. I spent those first days after spring break sitting in my room, wanting the past back. I was hurt by thoughts of what you did and I was upset by how much time and energy those thoughts and feelings consumed. But the grind of school and work couldn't be put on hold so I tried pushing it away once again. This time, it seemed impossible to suppress. I couldn't get it out of my mind.

I mentioned in passing to a close friend that I was struggling with recurrent memories of an encounter that had occurred a year ago and that I had been thinking more deeply about what had actually happened. I didn't really understand what I was thinking and feeling and felt unable to convey what was going on. Nothing really came of that or some other early conversations, but I kept reaching out to other friends. I felt I needed help in coping with this situation.

It finally took the right friend to understand what I was trying to express. As soon as I told her what I had been telling my other friends, she came over. She gave me the hug I needed and asked if I would tell her what I'd been thinking about. All I could really say was that I wasn't sure about what had happened and that I thought I was wrong about it being "just sex." She asked a few basic questions: "What do you mean when you say you were wrong about it being 'just sex'? What did he do and how did you feel about it?" These questions forced me to be honest with myself and understand what I was feeling. It felt good to finally talk meaningfully to someone.

I wanted to get to the point where I could talk openly about what you did, to be able to see a similar situation in a movie and not feel ill. I wanted to be able to cry about it and feel okay with myself again, to look in the mirror and feel pride instead of fear, hurt and self-doubt. I wanted to recover my spunk, to be able to have fun, and to be a friend again.

Little reminders of you and your actions kept popping up everywhere. One morning, I picked out a shirt that was the same color as the one I wore the night you raped me. I saw your friend in the cafeteria. I passed through your town on my drive home on a weekend trip. Violent sexual scenes from movies and TV shows reminded and scared me.

The summer came and I woke up from a nightmare one morning before work. In my dream, I had been raped and I dreamt that immediately afterwards, I was trying to tell someone what had happened. I was on the phone but something was preventing me from talking. It was as if someone were choking me; all the breath was taken from my lungs. I woke up in a panic. I didn't participate much at work that day. After work, my supervisor and a good friend asked if I'd run an errand with her. In the car she asked if something was bothering me. After some hesitation, I told her about my nightmares and what had happened to me. I felt sick to my stomach as I recounted the events and tried my best to distance myself from them. Yet my friend listened and I began to feel that I could safely talk about what you had done.

Opening up to friends was the key that unlocked months of suppressed emotion. I needed time by myself to sort out my feelings. I went to sit on the beach one afternoon and as I thought about things, I started to get angry. I was mad at you for taking advantage of my trust, for not listening to me. I was mad at myself for not saying "no" just one more time, as if all the times I did say "no" were not enough. (Shouldn't once have been enough?) I was mad for not getting up and leaving sooner. I struggled to understand how an encounter as brief as twenty minutes could completely change me.

As fate would have it, I saw you again. Do you remember that? After giving a campus tour, I was asked to help at the orientation for transfer students. As I was explaining materials to parents, I heard someone ask, "Am I in the right line?" I glanced up from my notes to find you looking me straight in the eye. A sudden wave of fear hit me as I instantly placed your face and voice. After getting your orientation materials, you found a seat. Did you pick that seat on purpose? The lights seemed to be shining directly on you, making the whole situation very surreal. I felt as though you were staring at me. Did you even know who I was? I realized what the ramifications were. You were going to be a student at the same university. I would probably see you on campus. You could be in one of my classes. We might even end up living in the same residence hall.

Throughout this period, a few of my friends suggested I talk to a professional, someone prepared to help a person in my situation. But I felt I could handle this on my own. Why did I need to talk to a professional? Did my friends think I wasn't strong enough? Eventually, I did let a friend take me to the counseling center, but I sat in the car for a good twenty minutes before I went in.

A few days later, I had an appointment with a counselor. I went into the session feeling very nervous. I sat down and didn't really know what to say. The counselor asked me to start the story wherever I felt comfortable. I couldn't even think straight, but I took a deep breath and tried to reassemble the pieces of that night. The counselor asked a few questions. I attempted to answer them, but my answers were halting and incomplete. She suggested I think about the questions after that day's session and try writing about them.

Think of a time you were caught off guard. How did it feel?

I tried to be stoic. I felt that if I said anything or even changed my expression, everyone would know what happened to me and I was not ready for that. I felt I had to be tough about it. If people talked about me or about what happened, if they made jokes, I was afraid I wouldn't be able to confront them.

If you were to talk about it, what would you say to others?

I think I would say that I'm uncomfortable even thinking about it, that it's something I'm dealing with and that it's something no one else should have to go through.

What helps you deal with it?

Since I'm not one to open up to just anyone, it really helps when people ask me about it and listen to what I have to say. I feel like I'm burdening people when I bring it up. My friends have enough to worry about; they don't need someone else's problems to deal with. It also really helps when people ask specific questions; it helps me work through this from a new direction.

What did you really lose?

I lost the possibility of sharing that experience for the first time. I lost trust in other people—I sometimes look at them and wonder what bad things they're thinking or doing. I feel I can't go anywhere without being afraid that he'll be there or that he'll find out where I live. I lost the ability to have fun; I lost my carefree attitude; I lost my innocence. I lost myself. He took that from me.

Writing answers to these questions was the beginning of my facing my rape head-on, and the counselor's questions helped me to focus directly on what happened and how it affected me. A week later, I left another session with more questions to explore:

If you saw him on campus and passing him was unavoidable, what would you do?

My instinct would be to walk right past him with my head down. Then again, that would suggest that I'm ashamed or embarrassed, which I guess I am. I shouldn't be; I know I shouldn't be, but I still feel that way. I would want to walk with my head up, look him straight in the eye, and stand my ground. I would want to be okay.

How did that night change the way you think of people?

I wonder about everyone and everything when I'm not in a completely familiar place with familiar people. I'm constantly checking behind my back nervously. I'm just not comfortable where I am. That uncertainty has become a part of me. It's not as though I'm conscious of it; it's just a part of my life now. I have to remember to relax. I don't feel I can trust people, especially guys. By taking away my innocence, he changed how I think of human beings altogether. I'd like to think people are good for the most part, but I'm no longer so sure.

What makes you uncomfortable?

Being alone around guys I don't know well. Jokes about rape. The word "rape." Situations where the topic is brought up, even when it doesn't directly concern me. When I see something similar in a movie or on TV. Hearing or saying his name. When I'm in a place with someone I don't want to be with. When there's no way out of something. When someone doesn't listen to what I say or how I feel. When a guy even flirts with me.

These questions opened a floodgate. I spent the next week sitting in my room, thinking, crying, and trying to understand. The whole thing just consumed me. I couldn't focus on homework, classes, or my job. I didn't care enough to put on a pair of jeans and a nice shirt; instead I wore pajama pants and sweatshirts all the time. I obsessed over finding answers any way I could—in books, websites, anyplace. Every day was a rollercoaster; I was a mess. Like the previous two, the third counseling session sparked more things to think about.

What happens when someone asks you about being raped?
What do you do?

I freeze up. I don't know why but I just stare. It's hard to open up about it. But if I don't, it's as if I'm trying to keep a secret. On the other hand, if I do tell people about the rape, it often makes them uncomfortable. They sometimes change the subject or just avoid it altogether. They don't understand that trying to avoid what happened is like denying a piece of who I am. Sometimes I wish people just knew what I was thinking. I wish people just knew that I needed a hug, someone to sit with and someone to tell me that everything's going to be okay. I wish people knew to keep asking questions instead of changing the subject, even if I do seem upset.

What's holding you back from telling your mom about what
happened?

I know my mom's going to be hurt that I haven't told her about what happened. She's going to think I didn't trust her enough. In the beginning, I didn't tell her because I was afraid of her reaction. I thought she would freak out and have me come home instantly. The last thing I need is for the rest of my life to change. I know she'll be upset knowing that someone hurt her daughter. I don't want that to be the topic of discussion every time I come home for a holiday break; holidays are for celebrating, not for crying. And I know she's going to want to talk about how she feels with one of her sisters. If I tell her, then there is a good chance that the whole family will know—all of my aunts, uncles, and cousins. Word travels fast in a big Roman Catholic family.

What's stopping you from moving on?

Everything I do seems to revolve around this one event. I don't understand how twenty minutes can have such an impact on a life, but it can. Part of me thinks that I shouldn't be so affected by it. I ask myself, "What's the big hold up? It's over." But it's not over. I haven't been going to class; I sit on my couch and think about it all day. It's taken all of my energy and focus. By the end of the day, I'm still thinking. I go to bed, try to sleep, then wake up and do it all over again.

Have you had any recurring dreams?

I had a certain dream for the third time a few nights ago. In this dream, my tooth got knocked out. I tried holding it in place so it could take root and grow back. It never did. What does that mean?

What do you think about guys?

About a year and a half ago, one of my best guy friends told me he loved me, before I fully realized how much I'd been affected by the night I was sexually assaulted. My friend kept telling me his feelings, but I kept turning him down. I just wasn't into it. He got mad and couldn't accept my answer, but eventually he gave up. We don't really talk anymore.

I find myself wishing for a committed relationship, seeing as I've never had one. I keep trying to force something. Any time a guy is interested, I try to make it work. We go on a date or hang out. But it never feels right. Is this how it's always going to be?

One night, while I was studying, my mom called. She sounded worried. She kept asking, "Are you okay?" I kept telling her I was. She told me she knew something was wrong. Someone—probably one of my siblings or my dad—read my instant messaging profile online and showed it to my mom. I guess she figured out from what was written that things weren't good here at school. She asked what happened. I told her I didn't know. She asked again. I couldn't answer. She guessed it. Moms just have a way of knowing things. We talked and cried on the phone for about an hour. She decided to fly up here two days later. I didn't understand why she wanted to be here; I knew I didn't want to talk about it with her. For three days, I showed her around the place I call home. One morning, we went to the bagel shop for breakfast. As we were sitting at the table in the front window, she asked, "So is everything okay?" I answered, "Yes." Then she asked, "You covered all your bases?" I knew what she was getting at. She wanted to know if I had gone to a doctor for an exam. I clenched my teeth and answered, "Yes," hating that I wasn't telling the truth. I know I should get checked out, but every time I go to make an appointment, I get scared. I don't want to be hurt like I hurt the night you raped me. Mom changed the subject and I was relieved. That's the last time we talked about it.

At my final appointment, my counselor said she thought it was cool that during the rape I was able to kick you off. I thought so too, but I still didn't understand why it took me so long to do it. What I didn't know is that there's more than just a "fight or flight" response; many women freeze. My counselor said this is because many women don't feel they're strong enough or fast enough to fight or flee. She said, "Women freeze to get through the situation alive. While there is an attack on a woman's body, she tries to numb her mind so it isn't attacked as well." She also said that the response is natural and doesn't imply consent. When she told me this, my whole body relaxed. I felt an enormous weight lift. I could breathe again. It was the first time I believed that it wasn't my fault.

I left my counseling appointment that day with a smile on my face. I drove home singing at the top of my lungs to my favorite song. I got to my room and called a close friend to ask if she'd meet me for breakfast. I was excited. Things were different. I was back. I ran into a classmate and gave her a huge hug. I went shopping with other friends and went to dinner with my mentor in the leadership program on campus. We were having great conversation. Then she asked why my mom had come up so suddenly. I was lost again; the butterflies turned into a knot in my stomach. Should I tell her what happened, why my mom really wanted to come up? I couldn't. That day, I felt as though my real self was back and then she was gone again.

I knew I had work to do. I started talking about what had happened and what I was feeling. I talked to every friend I knew. I talked to more people instead of unloading it all onto one person. Having seen a glimmer of my former self, I continued the quest—I had to. Sure, my life was still a rollercoaster, but the ups were higher and the downs weren't as low. I started feeling as if there was finally a light at the end of the tunnel.

And yes, I saw you, at one of the hockey games. I was with a big group of friends and so were you. You sat about six rows behind me. I felt you staring at me. I was scared the whole time. At one point, I glanced back and you were looking at me. I looked you straight in the eye and turned back around. That took guts. A friend with whom I had shared my experience could tell by the look on my face what was going on. She grabbed my hand, reassured me that everything would be okay and we sat and watched the rest of the game. I was so lucky I had friends with me. After the game, we waited a few minutes to be sure you were gone. Once I got home, I felt a little safer. I took some time for myself before I joined the group for a movie. I knew that I was okay.

Soon after that, I got an e-mail from a friend. Her boyfriend had recently had a few friends over to hang out. I wasn't there, but she said that one friend brought a guy along. This guy apparently started talking about the "fun and crazy times" he had at my school even before he became a student here. He was telling everyone (who, coincidentally, all knew me) about a girl he met and "had sex with." He mentioned seeing her at his campus orientation and at a hockey game. You were that guy. In your story, you called me by my nickname. My nickname is not a common one, and my friends knew you were talking about me. You DO remember me. You remember my face and my name. Do you remember all the times I said "No"? Do you remember my pushing you off of me?

I took a walk not long ago and thought about how far I have come. Although I feel more guarded and less carefree than I did before it happened, I also feel more aware. I place more value on friendship. I am more in tune with myself. I am better able to recognize when others are hurting. I still get excited about the little things in life, like I did before you hurt me. I am increasingly confident.

The consequences of your actions—the pain you caused—challenged me to find and understand myself. I am now closer to my friends and family. I've discovered an inner strength I never knew I had. I've realized that it's okay to not be okay. My faith was rocked, but I'm discovering a new relationship with God. I have discovered a lot. I have discovered me.

KAREN

In June 1994, I received a telephone call from a woman who claimed to have had a relationship with my husband Ron. When Ron came home, I confronted him and an argument followed. Later that night, the woman called again, wanting to know if I was "okay." She explained that Ron had been physically abusive to her on more than one occasion, and she worried that if I told him about our earlier conversation, he would hurt both of us. I could hear the fear in her voice. I was sitting on my bed at the time, wearing only a T-shirt and underwear, and my husband was next to me. I tried to keep the conversation from him, answering in monosyllables. But when I hung up the phone, I could see that Ron was angry. He looked at me with hatred in his eyes and said, "Oh, so the two of you are plotting against me? I ought to punch you in the face, break your jaw, and you can call and tell her all about it." I looked him straight in the eye and said evenly, "If you put your hands on me, it won't be her I'll be calling— it will be the police." He turned away from me and reached into the nightstand on his side of the bed. When he turned back, there was a knife in his hand. He put the knife up to my face and dared me to repeat what I had just said. I refused to answer him. After what seemed like an eternity, he turned away from me and put the knife back into the drawer. I lied and said that I had to go to the bathroom. I slid off the bed, reached for my pocketbook, and ran out of my apartment barefoot. I didn't stop running until I had reached the police station two blocks away. To this day, I don't know why Ron didn't follow me. I was a sight arriving at the police station dressed only in my T-shirt and underwear. I asked the police to return with me to my home. The front door was open, lights were on, Ron was gone and so was the knife. The next day, I went to Family Court and got an Order of Protection. The judge ordered that Ron be removed from the apartment. Later that day, the police came and escorted him from our home.

A few weeks later, I woke up on a sunny Saturday morning. When I opened my bedroom door, Ron was standing there, wearing only plaid boxer shorts. In his right hand was the same knife. In his left hand were two black ropes. He told me to lie down on the bed. When I said no, he punched me with a closed fist in the middle of my chest with such force that I was knocked backward onto the bed. He placed one of his knees on each of my upper arms, pinning me down. Using the black ropes, he tied my wrists to the headboard. When I started to cry and scream, he took the scarf off my head and stuffed it in my mouth. In my dresser drawer, he found a pair of black pantyhose, cut them in half with the knife and tied my ankles to the footboard. I was tied spread-eagle to my own bed, in my own home. He stepped out of his boxer shorts, climbed up onto the bed, cut off my underwear with the knife and raped me. I remember the actual rape as if I had been floating above my bed watching the scene from the ceiling. He kept jabbing at me with the knife, saying, "This is all your fault. You should have let me come home. What happens between a man and his wife is nobody's business." I thought, "If I move, the knife is going to slip and I will die."

After he raped me, he walked over to the hamper, pulled out a T-shirt and wiped himself off. I made myself pay attention to his every action, aware that I would need evidence. I looked at the VCR to see what time it was. I observed what clothes he was wearing and what kind of sneakers he put on. I watched everything he did.

Ron got dressed, removed my gag, and asked me where my pocketbook was; he wanted money. I lied and told him I'd left it at my girlfriend's house. I lied again when I said that I needed to call my girlfriend to tell her not to come over. I told him that we had made plans to go shopping that day and that I didn't want her to come to my house. He untied me and let me use the phone. I could not call for help as he stood over me with the knife while I made the phone call. I called my best friend and told her not to come over. Of course, she had no idea what I was talking about, but she could tell that I was crying. When she asked me if I was all right, I said, "No." Intuitively, she asked me if Ron was there. I said, "Yes," and she asked to speak to him on the phone. I gave the phone to him and moved away from the bed. I couldn't hear all that he said to her, but I could see that he was crying too.

While Ron spoke on the phone, I thought about ways to escape. But my front door locked from the inside with a key and the key was in my pocketbook in the closet. It would have been impossible to run to the closet, find my key, unlock the door, and escape without Ron catching up to me. And he still had that knife.

I simply moved away from him. After he hung up the phone, he turned to me and asked if I were okay. This angered me as much as the rape did. I remember saying, "You will have to kill me before I ever let you touch me again." He simply laughed and went downstairs into the kitchen. When I heard him open the refrigerator door, I picked up the phone and called 911. I remember whispering hysterically into the phone, "My husband is in my house, he raped me, he has a knife, please send the police." The 911 operator was calm. She asked all the appropriate questions and tried to calm me down. She told me several times not to hang up, that the police were on their way. When I heard a door slam shut, I panicked and hung up the phone. I never told the operator who I was or where I lived!

Within two minutes, the police arrived. Ron had run out the back door. I remembered that a red light on my kitchen telephone lights up whenever another extension is in use. Ron must have seen the light and known that I was calling the police. Five minutes after the police arrived, I heard a car door slam and the police say, "I'm sorry, ma'am, but you can't go in there. It's a crime scene." I heard my best friend's voice, and I was able to convince the police to let her come in.

As a nurse, I knew the importance of immediate medical care and evidence collection after a rape. I showed the police the ropes and pantyhose that were still tied to the bed. I showed them the T-shirt Ron had used to wipe himself off. Finally, the police let my friend take me to the hospital.

At the time of the assault, I was the head nurse of an emergency department near my home. I decided not to go to the hospital where I worked because I didn't want my staff to have to do a rape exam on their supervisor. Instead, I went to another local hospital where I was immediately left alone in a cubicle. The doctor who came to examine me did not speak to me or acknowledge my presence. He walked over to the counter, picked up the Rape Kit and began to read the directions. I knew then that I was in trouble. I convinced the doctor to let me show him how to use the kit since I had assisted with several rape exams in the past. That's right—I had to show the doctor how to collect my own evidence!

The few months after the rape were the worst of my life. I thought they would never catch Ron and, even if they did, I believed he would never be convicted. To this day, many people don't believe that a husband can be guilty of rape against his wife. It was a long time before I regained my appetite and was able to get a good night's sleep. I still can't sleep without the TV on. I am afraid of the silence. I set the timer so that the TV goes off long after I am asleep.

I was lucky that my husband was eventually brought to trial. During the trial, he was arrested for criminal possession of a controlled substance and a bargain was struck: he pleaded guilty to first degree rape in order to get a reduced sentence on both charges. Just before I was due to take the stand to testify, he changed his plea from "not guilty" to "guilty" and was subsequently sentenced to three to nine years in May of 1995. Ron went to prison in August of that year. He came before the parole board three times but was denied parole each time. After serving seven of the nine years in prison, Ron was released in the spring of 2002, and he was released from parole last year after completing the remaining two years of his sentence as a parolee. Because he is free, I am often asked why I choose to remain in the same house in the same city. I do so because I have resolved not to give him any more power over my life. My friends and family are here. My life is here and I love my job. He will not make me flee.

The rape and its aftermath gave me the will, strength, and ability to become an advocate for other survivors. As a result of my experience at the hospital, I became trained as a Forensic Nurse Examiner and I now coordinate the local Sexual Assault Nurse Examiner (SANE) Program. A SANE nurse is a specially trained RN who provides an objective, comprehensive assessment of patients who report that they have been raped or sexually assaulted. In addition, we oversee the collection of physical evidence from the victim's body. We are experts in providing care for these very special patients. We also provide expert testimony in court about the evidence collection process and any injuries that we documented. I have made it my mission to see that no patient in my county is re-victimized by the medical exam that occurs in the hospital.

My commitment to direct service and advocacy encompasses both my private and professional lives. In addition to seeing patients in a clinical setting, I work for a non-profit, community-based organization that provides a wide range of services to victims of crime, including community outreach and Rape Awareness Education. I volunteer for numerous local, state, and international organizations and have recently joined a local Sexual Assault Response Team, that provides forensic examiners to public hospitals in my area. Not only do such programs provide compassionate care for sexual assault victims, they are instrumental in helping to hold perpetrators accountable for their actions.

In addition, my outreach work allows me to educate others about sexual assault, forensic nursing, and related topics. I have appeared on television talk shows and in film documentaries. I have testified before Congress and appeared before State and Federal agencies.

Tragedy can be turned into triumph. Survivors of sexual assault can and must be heard—through poetry, art, music, or public speaking. We can each work toward prevention of sexual assault and we can provide support for victims in our own way—by volunteering in a shelter, on a hotline, or perhaps by pursuing a career in medicine, law, or social services. In a culture where rape depends on a conspiracy of silence, survivors who speak out heal more than themselves.

DONNA

There are times I believe we live in a culture that accepts, even encourages, assault—a rape culture. Men, and some women, cross intimate boundaries with practiced indifference. It seems "no" is not a warning, just a mile marker. How many women, like myself, can count the number of times they have been assaulted? Because we are not openly educated about what assault is or how we should respond, for ourselves or for others, there are repeat offenders and repeat victims.

It was a warm summer day in Chicago. I was twenty-two. I had ridden to Grant Park on my new Peugeot bicycle, a graduation present. The ride was over 60 blocks, but I loved the exercise. As the day waned and I hung out with folks in the park, I dreaded the long ride home. One of the people I met, a taller gentleman, offered to give me a lift to the South Side. I accepted. I had four brothers and was used to being around young guys without incident. So we took off my quick release wheels, stored them in the trunk of his car and sped off. When we got to about Eighty-seventh Street, he said he needed to stop at his apartment briefly. He invited me inside and offered me some juice. As I finished the juice, he grabbed my arm and would not let go. He was much bigger than I am and had a menacing, deadly serious glare. Then he raped me. I believe that if I had struggled, I would not be alive. I told some friends, including my boyfriend. He was alarmed and angry. I did not tell the police, nor did I tell my mom or dad. Demanding justice wasn't part of the equation. Dad was an alcoholic batterer who had started molesting me at age twelve. Mom was getting beaten by him so often that she scarcely had energy for me. I was the good girl who brought home A's and B's and tiptoed around the violence. I was not about to create a scene. I could live with it—I already had. If my story ended there, it would have been enough. But it does not.

A year later I went to graduate school out of state to bury my troubles and make my way. I was doing well . . . until one night in my second floor apartment. I had just completed my master's degree and was celebrating with friends. My classmates had come to say farewell. The last one to leave leaned over to congratulate me with a kiss. I turned my head. Then it happened. He pinned me to the floor. He was moaning and panting. I could smell the liquor on his breath. I was shocked, angry, and scared. I crossed my legs and pleaded, "No, no, no, do not do this." His musty, intoxicated breath nauseated me. I struggled, but he was too strong, too heavy. He pulled down my pants and forced himself inside. I found myself worrying that if I moved, the huge philodendron might fall on top of me and knock me out. I could not get up. Then he finished. It happened so fast. Suddenly, he picked me up and tried to carry me to the bedroom. "Oh no," I thought, "he is going to do it again!" I struggled harder, fighting and clawing. My bike fell over. I ran out of the house half-dressed and hid like an animal, crouching in the bushes. It seemed like hours passed. Then I ran wildly, knocking on doors and asking for help. The first person I found was one of my rapist's friends. Somewhat incoherently, I tried to explain what had happened. His friend, only half awake, was unresponsive. I ran away, looking for a someone who would help. Another door opened. This time, I found a friend of my own. "What's wrong?" he asked. My hair was a mess, my face streaked with tears. He and another friend drove me to the emergency room. The nurse performed a rape exam, snipping, cutting, asking, bagging. It was 1:30 in the morning. I was cold. The party had ended and the nightmare had begun.

I was so angry. I wanted to press charges. The rapist's best friend threatened to lie on the witness stand about me if I did not drop it. My friends told me how brave I would be to just let things go—they thought they were doing the right thing. I wish I'd had an advocate back then, someone to help me examine my choices, to support me for the fight, someone to tell me that rapists don't stop raping until they are stopped. I had what police call "a good rape case." That is, I had gone immediately to the ER, the hospital had collected DNA evidence, and I had heard of another victim who had been raped by the same man. But in those first few hours and weeks, there was no informed person to help me figure out what to do. No rape crisis counselor called. Even the prosecutor did not try to press me.

I moved away and began working on my career. Two years later I got married. Then I started to wake in the night, screaming. My husband had to shake me awake to let me know I was okay. Still, I did not go to counseling. I stuffed my emotions, continued to receive job promotions and moved up North. Seven years passed.

Things started getting worse, especially after the birth of our child. My husband went to counseling but I did not want to go. I figured that since the rapist was out of my life and my dad was out of my life, there was nothing to talk about. But the trauma was oozing out of me, little by little. My husband was adamant that I try counseling. One day I got a phone call from our pastor's secretary who wanted to set up an appointment for me. I thought to myself, "I will go, but I am not staying." But when I got there, the pastor was charming and seemed compassionate. I relaxed and felt I could let down my guard. Each week, in an empty building, late at night, we met for counseling sessions. When I talked to him about how I didn't like to be touched, a telling sign of incest or rape trauma, his response was to give me assignments involving explicit sexual material. He shared personal information about his marriage. He told me about his wife's sexual issues and his own sexual exploits. He made sexual jokes and innuendoes. I did not know what to make of this unorthodox counseling. In retrospect, I see that I was being groomed for hands-on offenses. He was testing my boundaries and my sense of reality to see if I would complain. I was a victim in waiting. Our culture had taught me to trust professionals, especially our clergy. So I did.

His actions became more intrusive: what began as innuendo became long-lasting, full-bodied hugs. When I did not seem resistant, he counseled me that phone sex was therapeutic. He took to verbal assaults, then he moved on to abusive actions that he claimed were signs of "intimacy"—fondling, exposing his genitals, and digital penetration.

After nearly fifty hands-on sexual assaults, I was devastated. This criminal had ripped my heart and soul from me and thrown them at my feet. Not surprisingly, I was not the only "patient" he was "counseling." When another of his victims taped his phone messages, the cat was out of the bag. I discovered later that he had raped her too. I felt as if I had been cut in half with a pair of scissors. I was depressed. I had flashbacks and intrusive, sometimes suicidal thoughts. I was a wreck. How was I to heal? How could I get help? Miraculously, I did heal. One small step at a time. I interviewed and re-interviewed therapists. I read everything I could get my hands on: *Courage to Heal, Strong at the Broken Places, Secret Survivors, Sexual Involvement with Therapists, Patients as Victims, Sex in the Forbidden Zone, I Never Called It Rape, The Date Rape Prevention Book, The Other Side of Silence,* and *Dangerous Relationships,* to name a few. I needed to understand what had happened and why. I went to individual and group therapy and cried the poison of sexual assault out of my system one session at a time.

I also filed a civil suit. This was a huge step for me. As an adult child of an alcoholic batterer, I was scared to stand up for myself because I thought no one would believe me. A therapist said to me, "If you never learn to stand up for yourself, you will always feel like someone's victim." I determined that I would see the civil suit through. Besides, it was not me that had to prevail. It was the law.

Knees shaking, I went to the sex crimes unit to report the sexual abuse I had experienced at the hands of my pastor. I thought, "They will laugh at me. Here I am, forty years old with a master's degree. Who will believe that this has happened to me?" But the personnel in sex crimes did believe me. When I discovered that my state did not have laws to put Reverend Rapist in jail, I contacted my state legislator and together we drafted new legislation. That was in 1997. A stakeholders' meeting, several drafts, and many hearings later, the law was enacted in 2001. The jig was up in my state for predatory therapists.

When my pastor stalked me, I got a personal protection order. Some of my story appeared in print. A reader who had been raped by her pastor read it and contacted me. A year later, her pastor was ousted and she won her lawsuit. Other victims came forward to prosecute abusers and get their personal lives back on track.

To Reverend Rapist, I became the Victim from Hell. He would think twice before he raped again. Yet, even so, I am still chilled when I recall this man, in a clergy collar, insisting that he was doing God's will, that it was for my benefit, that it was "healing." I experienced some self-doubt for a time. I had known how to fight off the rapist in my college apartment. But when my own pastor said this was healing, how could I fight back?

That is why I became an advocate. This is my fight. I have been featured on television shows and radio shows for one purpose—to stop violence against the vulnerable.

Judith Herman, author of the classic *Trauma and Recovery*, writes that we must reclaim our past when we work through trauma. We need to do things we left undone and pursue things we might only have dreamed about. . . . That is what I have finally done, I revel in my personal and professional success, making films about music, the arts, love stories, and more. I love playing golf with my husband and my son, showing off my 13 handicap, and directing musicals that help kids ignite their souls . . . and I continue to speak on mental health issues and rape prevention.

And I laugh and laugh and laugh. When you meet me, you can't tell that I have been through this and so much more. There are times I wish, however, that I was a non-raped woman. I wish that my spouse did not have to deal with all that pain. But then I get a call from a married woman who was raped by a pastor. The only man she had ever been intimate with was her husband, until she met her own local Reverend Rapist. We talk for hours. I make her laugh, a sentiment she did not think was possible. I connect her with lawyers, with therapists, with people who can help her put her life back together. I see that it is all worth it.

One of my deepest lessons comes from *The Wizard of Oz*. When the evil monkeys attack the scarecrow in the haunted forest, his insides are ripped away. A leg is over there, an arm is someplace else, but his friends come and put his stuffing back in. It is my friends who have helped me put my stuffing back in—stuffing that was ripped out by incest, by multiple rapes, by predators. And my friends have been many: authors of books, filmmakers, children who sang songs, ballerinas on point, and always, always my family, my spouse, and my son.

GABRIEL

Most people think that rape or sexual assault affects only women, but that is a myth. I am a male survivor of sexual assault. I was molested between the ages of twelve and nineteen by a very close and trusted friend of the family. He was so close to our family that my brothers, cousins, and I considered him an uncle. He was my older sister's date to a winter formal. He worked as Santa Claus at a local mall during Christmastime. I never thought that anybody in my family would believe me if I told them what he was doing to me. But it went on year after year.

In February 2001, when I was nineteen, I went to the hospital to visit a family member who was on a ventilator in the final stages of muscular dystrophy. I was sitting with him while he was asleep. Our family friend came in and tried to force himself on me again. This time he was thwarted by the ventilator alarms, which summoned the nursing staff. That was the last time he laid his hands on me. That night, I returned to my aunt's house and told my family what had happened. I was scared, but I wanted it to stop, and I wanted people to know what had been happening all those years. I called my grandmother and told her. Finally, I went home and told my mom. We both cried. I went to the police department and waited for an officer to take a report. As I sat out in the cold February air, about a million thoughts ran through my head. What if they didn't believe me? What was I going to say? Finally, an officer pulled up and I was relieved to see that it was a woman. I was afraid that a male officer wouldn't take me seriously. By 7:30 the next morning, the report was filed, the family friend had confessed and been arrested, and I was finally on my way home for some sleep. One by one, family members found out. Most of them expressed shock and disbelief. Many people wanted to talk to me about what had happened and I told them. Some believed me and some did not.

The trial was a very painful experience for everyone. Because this man had such close ties to my family, his plea of not guilty literally split my family in two. It pitted sibling against sibling, blood against blood. To this day, some members of my family won't speak to me.

Around the time of the preliminary hearing, I began counseling at the local YWCA. I talked about my concerns, my family, and what was bothering me. It helped a lot, but I was dismayed to find that there were not very many agencies that were equipped to meet the needs of male victims. Some agencies or hotlines I called would hang up as soon as they heard a male voice on the other end of the line. Most simply said that they only assisted women. This was very frustrating. So I began to keep a journal. I didn't write in it every day, but I wrote in it whenever something important happened or if I felt I needed to get something off my chest. The biggest relief was actually being able to talk about what had happened to me. I had been silent for so many years. I had kept that suffocating secret for so long. Each time I talked or wrote about it, I felt as though I gained a little piece of myself back.

As a gay man, I am still asked if I feel that my sexual orientation stems from my sexual abuse as a child, and I have also found that a common fear among male victims is that what happened might somehow make them gay. I understand that many people think this, but I certainly don't. Just because a member of the same sex does something to you does not make you a homosexual. Being molested did not make me gay, it made me hurt and isolated. My personal belief is that people have no control over their sexual orientation, just like their eye color, hair color, etc. Sexuality is not something that someone can force on you, or take away from you. I have also learned that sexual assault has little or nothing to do with the personal aspects of the victim; it can happen to anyone regardless of age, gender or sexual orientation.

The trial took over a year. In that span of time, my relative with muscular dystrophy passed away, I left the person I was dating, and my family became more and more polarized. Some of my relatives made it very clear that they no longer would have anything to do with me. In fact, they did whatever they could to make my life absolutely miserable. During this difficult time, I realized that family is who you choose it to be. I chose to include in my family those people who were closest to me: my mother, my grandmother, my aunts, one of my brothers, my sister, an uncle, and several very close friends. With a family like that, I didn't miss quite so much the blood relatives I had lost.

For the trial, I had to produce character witnesses because the defense was attacking my credibility and character. I explained to former teachers, employers, and friends what was going on. I was surprised at how many people jumped at the opportunity to help me out. I didn't think that very many people would want to be a part of a trial like this. I was surprised and gratified to have so many people respond to my request for help.

On the last day of the trial, I was extremely nervous. A few final testimonies were given. One testimony came from my ex-boyfriend who, after our breakup, decided to testify against me in court. Witnesses were excluded from this phase of the trial, so I waited outside the courtroom. When all the testimonies were finished, I was allowed back inside. This day was the culmination of everything that had happened in the past year and four months. The man who molested me expected to be found innocent. I heard him describing to his mother the party they were planning that afternoon for when he was exonerated. He talked about the music he had burned onto a CD and the food he had bought. Then we heard closing arguments from both sides. I held my head up high even while the defense attorney portrayed me as a liar and a fake. Finally, both sides rested. The verdict came in. He was found guilty of twenty-one felony charges. I was sitting between my mom and my grandma. I turned to my mom and hugged her and cried. Then I hugged my grandma and my two aunts who sat behind me. I hugged my two best friends who had come to show their support. With all of the ruckus, I was sorry to miss seeing him handcuffed and taken into custody. But I would have another chance.

The sentencing hearing came about a month after the verdict was read. This was the time that people on both sides could read or present their impact statements to the court. My mother, my two aunts, and I read ours to the court. When we finished, the judge imposed a sentence of fifteen years and eight months in prison. The judge said the most damning testimony in the whole case was the defendant's own confession. My head was spinning. I held my grandmother's hand so tightly that my knuckles turned white, but I didn't avert my gaze. I saw the bailiff handcuff him. I saw his mother hit one of the deputies with her walker when he wouldn't let her give him a hug. After that I remember a lot of shouting coming from the other side of the courtroom. I don't remember much else, but that night, I slept better than I had in quite some time.

Not long after, the case came up for appeal. I only found out about it when the District Attorney called me with the results. The appeal had failed. Out of curiosity, I went to the courthouse to review the record of the case. The appeal had been based on the testimony of my ex-boyfriend (who had been discredited on the stand at the initial trial). But in the end, the State Appellate Court upheld both the conviction and the sentence. That was such a relief.

The nightmares and flashbacks have stopped. But some wounds just heal more slowly than others. I am working on these. Recently, I went to the State of California Megan's Law website and typed in his name. There he was—in a full color picture. Underneath his photograph in big red, bold letters, it said "INCARCERATED." It's hard to describe the feelings that ran through me when I saw that word.

I felt relief, confirmation, joy, fear and anxiety all wrapped up in one huge emotion.

Throughout the trial, I continued my counseling sessions with the YWCA. It was the only agency that was willing to help me. It didn't matter to them that I was a man. They welcomed me and helped me to process the trauma I'd been through. One day my counselor asked me if I would be comfortable speaking to a group of new rape crisis hotline volunteers to tell them my story and I agreed to do it. I spoke for a brief time then quickly left. A few days later, I received an e-mail from my counselor who told me that because of what I had said at that training session, one of the volunteers had come forward to her family about her own sexual abuse. That was a very empowering experience for me. If what I had shared had impacted another person in a positive way, then why not do it more often? I enrolled in the next volunteer training session and subsequently became a rape crisis counselor and victim advocate.

Since then, I have spoken publicly numerous times about my experiences. And I have tried to raise awareness of the prevalence of male victims as well as female victims. I tell my story every chance I get, hoping that it may help someone else begin to heal. I still work the hotline for the rape crisis center. I live my life now knowing that what I have to say can make a difference, both in my own life and in the lives of others. I am not afraid to speak up anymore because my voice was heard and believed. I have even begun to mend some of the relationships that were torn apart when I first came forward. I am speaking again to my other brother and to other members of my family who hadn't believed me. And some of us are getting along again. That feels good. There are others with whom I may never be reconciled, but I have accepted that. Most importantly, I feel that justice was served. I feel whole again.

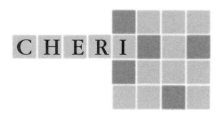

CHERI

I don't think anyone ever wakes up thinking they will be raped. It is a life changing experience. It has been fifteen years since I was raped at knifepoint in my apartment. I am a rape survivor, but there is more to "survival" than simply coming out of the attack alive. Survival is a process that molds you into the person that you will become. I am very proud of who I am, and I owe so much of that to my family and friends.

Rape does not just affect the survivor. It affects everyone in the survivor's life—family, friends, and co-workers. It changes everyone. Just moments after the attack, I called my dad and told him I had been raped. I cannot describe the looks upon my parents' faces as they walked into the hospital room. As they hugged me, my dad was shaking and teary-eyed. I'll never forget that. I had rarely seen my mom cry and never my dad.

Once they saw me, I think they felt better. I wasn't battered or cut and had no broken bones. My mom described how my dad had picked her up from work and driven her the thirty minutes to the hospital. She was shaken by the look on my dad's face as he told her what had happened. That was very difficult to hear.

When it was time to talk with the police, I wanted my mom with me. She was strong and I needed that. She sat with me as I described the rape in graphic detail to the officers. At the time, I felt I couldn't have my dad hear the details.

I have a very close family and the rape was hurting us all. Although I was very open about my feelings, I was extremely uncomfortable telling my dad the graphic details of what happened. In the first days after my rape, he was very quiet and even shut his friends out. One of the most difficult decisions I had to make was whether I wanted my dad to be present in the courtroom at the preliminary hearing. I didn't think I could graphically describe the rape in front of him. He told me that he would do whatever made me comfortable. My counselor felt he should be there, that it would help us both heal if Dad heard the whole story from me rather than from the newspapers.

So my dad and I took a drive and I talked about what had happened to me. That was so hard. I was hurt from the attack, physically and emotionally, but he was in a lot of pain too. We were both very emotional and my dad just held my hand while I told him all of the inaccuracies in the newspaper report. He shared that he and mom felt so helpless. They knew they could not take my pain away and that was extremely difficult for them. I still cry just thinking about that moment. My counselor was right. My dad needed to hear the details from me; it prevented him from imagining things that didn't happen.

The preliminary hearing was ten days after my rape and my Dad did attend. Afterward, I felt like my dad was back. The family was able to laugh again and we all needed that. Some of the questions asked in court are so ridiculous that you can't do anything but laugh. At least we could laugh together.

Not only were my parents affected, but also my siblings, my friends, and my co-workers. My sister felt guilty. She had helped me to find my apartment and had lived for a while in the same complex. She blamed herself for the rape. I never blamed her, but she had a hard time dealing with both the guilt and the rape. My brother was away at college and was asked not to talk to anyone about the assault or the court case. Because he has always been open about his feelings, keeping everything inside was very tough for him. He ended up transferring to the university in our hometown. I was glad to have him home and I think it helped him to heal too.

The most important part of my recovery was having my family with me; they were always supportive and available to talk. At the same time, it was important to know that we didn't always have to talk about the attack. It wasn't exactly an easy topic of conversation. I could talk about it when I needed to, but it was also good to know that we didn't have to dwell on it each time we were together. Just the presence of my family was comforting. When a survivor is ready, she will talk. And, when she does, be ready. There are a lot of feelings and emotions. Some will make sense and some won't. None of them are wrong.

I went to counseling immediately following my rape. In addition to the support from my family, I needed to talk to a professional. I had thoughts and emotions that no one could fully understand and since my family was going through so much pain of their own, I felt these feelings might just hurt them more. All of my dreams were about the rapist. I visualized hurting him, which was very difficult and strange for me. It was so much better to express my thoughts to someone who wasn't attached to the situation. I urge all survivors to seek professional counseling.

Even my co-workers were affected: things changed at the bank where both my sister and I worked. I was attacked in the morning, just as I was leaving for work. I never showed up. My colleagues, including my sister, assumed I was working at another branch that day. Some of the employees thought that I went to an out-of-town meeting with my boss. After the rapist left my apartment, I tried reaching my parents and my sister, Rita. I needed to have my family with me. I needed to feel safe. The first person I reached was Rita at work. Initially the employees at the bank couldn't recognize my voice because I was crying. Once I identified myself, they brought Rita to the back room, thinking I had been in an accident. When she got on the phone, I yelled, "I'VE BEEN RAPED." She didn't understand me, so I repeated it. Visibly pregnant, she ran through the bank as she left to come to me. Within an hour of my sister running out, the employees heard the radio announcement that a rape had occurred on the east side of town. They knew it was me.

In the first days after the rape, the bank brought in a counselor to talk to the employees and set up a "safety" system, which established that if an employee did not show up for work and did not call in sick, then someone would call that person to check on him or her. I think some of my sister's guilt came from knowing that she had been about to call me that morning to find out where I was, but just as she picked up the phone, a customer required her assistance and she never made the call. This single event opened so many eyes that morning. It raised awareness among my colleagues about the reality of rape. Such an occurrence has the chilling effect of reminding people that rape can happen to anyone.

At work, I was moved out of the public eye. The employees knew all too well what had happened from the newspapers (even though it was inaccurately reported). Nothing was hidden and I definitely believe that helped me. My co-workers handled it very well, and while I felt uncomfortable, I was not ashamed—I had no control over what had happened. The unwavering support I received from family, friends, and co-workers is the biggest reason I was able to move on with my life and work through this ordeal. However, I still had recovering to do on my own. I wondered if I would ever feel secure again. When I was by myself, I was scared. I turned on every light in the house and slept with the TV on so I wouldn't hear the noises in my home. I had to force myself to go outside alone. I told the members of my family to continue with their plans and that I would be okay. It was stretching the truth, but I knew I couldn't live in a shell and be protected forever. I felt I had to move on with my life. As time went by, things became easier to handle. I still keep lights on when I'm alone, and I sleep to a TV. It's just a comfort thing. After something like this happens, you will always be more aware of your surroundings, which is not a bad thing.

At the time of my rape, I was a swimming coach. Most of my teenaged athletes did not know about my rape. At competitions, athletes on my team sometimes made playful comments about trying to set me up with other coaches. That was not comfortable for me. I constantly turned down their attempts to play matchmaker. Once a swimmer even made a comment questioning my sexual orientation. I knew he was kidding, but I felt it was time to share with him what had happened. He was very understanding and refrained from future comments. If I feel my athletes are old enough and the moment is right, I will share my experience with a few of them. Since many young people take it for granted that nothing will happen to them, it's a reality check when they learn that someone they know and respect has been raped.

After the rape, it was a real challenge for me to trust men. I was a 23-year-old virgin with limited dating experience. It helped that some of my best friends were men. I knew they would not hurt me, but I did wonder sometimes if I would ever meet anyone, fall in love, and have a family. At the time of my rape, I had a very good male friend whom I loved and fully trusted. I received a lot of comfort from that relationship. We were able to hug and snuggle, but we never kissed or pursued a physical relationship. It was very easy to be with him—I knew I would not be hurt. That relationship helped me to move on. I believe in people establishing a friendship before they become lovers, especially when one is struggling with issues of trust. I think the types of relationships that last the longest are those in which both partners want to be together even when they know the best and the worst about one another.

Before my husband and I started dating, we were best friends. He knew of my rape and never pushed me to do anything sexually. He made suggestions, but didn't push. He waited until I was ready. That was wonderful. I was always a little scared, but I wanted to try things with the man I loved. When I thought of intimacy, I could recall only physical pain, so I was afraid of everything. I was even afraid of being kissed! That changed pretty quickly when I had so much fun kissing him!

I believe things happen for a reason. For some reason, I was raped. For some reason, I was a person who would live through it and move on. And now I am proof that there definitely can be a crazy, happy, fulfilling life after rape. Some wonderful events have occurred as a result of my rape. That's right! I said WONDERFUL things. For one, I met my wonderful husband who is also an awesome father, and we have five crazy, wild, and loving children. In addition, with help early on from my husband, my brother has become a nationally renowned speaker on sexual assault. Through his programs, he has had a positive impact on the lives of others—preventing some from experiencing such a horrendous ordeal themselves. For that, I know I was meant to be a survivor.

Recovering from a rape is a long and often difficult process, but walk away knowing that it was NOT your fault. I did. I knew I had done nothing wrong. I knew that my attacker had problems, that someone wouldn't ordinarily do this to another person. It helped that my attacker was jailed immediately (and later sent to prison). I often think about what I will do when I find out he's out of prison. I have three daughters who will be teenagers when he gets out. I plan to tell them when the time is right. I am comfortable with that thought.

Every so often, I think about my rape, especially when I see an assault portrayed on TV or in the movies, but I'm way too busy to dwell on it. I don't let it control my thoughts and actions. And believe it or not, I would not change anything in my past. My life experiences have molded me into the person I am today. And I am proud of who I am. I have a loving family, great friends, and an awesome job. I own my own business and run another, both very successfully.

Believe and trust in yourself and know that being raped, although devastating, is a single, uncontrollable event in your life. Move on with life the best way you know how, and live life to the fullest!

JULIETTE

On a Saturday night at the end of my first year of college, my friends and I went out to our favorite club. I had not been anxious to go out lately because I was still upset over my first true love breaking my heart only two months before. But my friends convinced me that I needed to start having fun and forget about him, so I took their advice and joined them for the evening.

Our group of ten arrived and walked into the best party of the year. Everyone in the club, including me, was dancing and having fun. Since there were only about 2,400 students at our school, I knew or recognized just about everyone there. I spotted an attractive guy that I had met only once in a friend's room a few months before. He recognized me as well and introduced himself. We danced and exchanged small talk about what we were studying and where we were from. He was polite and I felt comfortable with him. Throughout the course of the evening, we continued to dance and talk. We even kissed a couple of times.

As the night was winding down, I could see that he was intoxicated, although I'd had only two beers. When everyone began to leave the club, he invited me back to his room. I did enjoy his company and thought it would be fun to hang out with him just a little longer. At the same time, I was aware of what could happen to me if I went to an all-male dormitory after hours. So before I invited him to my place, I decided to do a background check on him. I asked my friends what they knew about this guy. Everyone had good things to say about him except for one girl who told me that she had heard he was a violent drunk. But another girl jumped into the conversation and reassured me that it was just a rumor and that she knew him very well from her hometown. Overall, I felt okay about the situation and invited him over to my dorm where we could be with all of my friends.

Unfortunately, when the cab dropped us off at my dorm, my friends were so intoxicated that all of them went to their own rooms and passed out, leaving me alone with my date. At this point, I began to feel uncomfortable because I did not know him well and I had lost the security that I thought my friends' presence would provide. He made friendly jokes about my friends and suggested we go up to my room and see what they were doing on the third floor. I knew that my roommate would be in our room, so even if no one else was hanging out on the third floor, at least we would not be alone. We went up, but found no one around. To make matters worse, as soon as I walked into my room with a date, my roommate assumed that we wanted to be alone. I asked her to stay, but she thought I was just trying to be polite and made a quick exit.

He sat on my bed and began to kiss me, but this time I did not enjoy it as much as I had before. I pulled away and tried to talk to him, but he had other plans. I could tell by the look in his eyes and the way that he was grabbing me that I was in a danger. I told him to let go of me and to stop grabbing me so forcefully. In seconds, he had managed to take off my shirt and overalls and everything underneath, as well as his own clothing—it seemed he had done this before. I remembered the words of the girl who said he was a violent drunk and I was terrified. He was bigger than I was, he was stronger than I was, and I was too afraid to scream. He began touching my body in ways that made me cringe. I begged him, "No! Stop! Please." He did not listen and proceeded to penetrate me. I told him "No!" again. He began to curse at me and screamed, "You don't want to fucking have sex with me?" When I cried, "No, not at all," he called me a bitch and then he smacked me on my right thigh. I tried to lock my legs together and use my hands to push him away. I did get him to stop having vaginal intercourse with me, however I sometimes wish that I had let him continue so as to get it over with because, for the next hour and a half, what I experienced was a bigger nightmare than I ever could have imagined. I put up as much of a fight as I could, but I didn't scream because I was afraid of what else he would do to me. He continued to sexually and physically abuse my body in every way he could. To this man, stop meant more, and tears meant I liked it.

When he finally left that evening, I did not feel much of anything, not even the developing bruises I had on my chest, legs and arms. I sat on my bed feeling numb. When my roommate came back, I began to tell her what had happened and she cried, telling me that I had just been raped. Strangely, I did not believe her—that could never happen to me, I thought to myself. I am a strong-minded woman who would never fall for a guy's game. However, I did not feel right in any sense of the word. I felt that my mind and body had been completely violated.

At first, I told only my three closest friends. They urged me to press charges, but I didn't think I could. I truly felt that I was somehow exaggerating. I thought that it could not be as serious as my friends believed, even though I had been very clear about saying no and he had chosen to ignore my requests. The more I flashed back to that night, the more I began to find strength within myself to report the rape. I knew that I had two options: to tell the city police and go through a long criminal trial where I might face being victimized by a defense attorney and the news media, while my assailant would likely be found innocent, as so often happens in rape cases; or I could report it to school security where the trial would be resolved more quickly and with less publicity. I chose to report the crime to the college in hopes that my assailant would be removed from the campus as soon as possible. The Office of Residential Life told me the hearing would be in one month.

In the month before the campus administrative hearing, I did some investigating of this man on my own. By asking around, I discovered that he had been a student at the school for only two months and in that short time, he had sexually assaulted at least three other women, all of whom told me of their assaults. The women agreed to tell the dean of students, who would be the deciding "judge" in the administrative hearing. At the hearing, my assailant told three different versions of what had happened. Meanwhile, I stuck to my story consistently, never wavering from the detailed security report in which I had first described the assault. There was only one true account of what happened that spring night in 1995, and it was obvious to everyone that it was mine.

Found guilty of both sexual and physical abuse by the administration, my attacker was given an insignificant punishment: social probation for one year. The college allowed him to continue to represent our school as an athlete and he was allowed to continue living on campus. The administration asked only that he not be involved in student government. They told him not to do it again and suggested that maybe he should seek some sort of counseling. Then we were dismissed.

Needless to say, I was appalled at the minimal sanction. I spent the next six months writing to the school newspaper. I spoke with the vice-president of the college and the dean of students who both responded in the same way: "He is not a threat to the campus community, Juliette. Now let's keep quiet about this!" I began to tell everyone I knew about the assault and the college's lenient response. I didn't care that the school had tried to silence me. I was determined to tell the truth. To add insult to injury, I was faced with my attacker every day after the assault—every single day—unless I decided to stay in my room, which I often did. Even though I was the victim of a violent assault, I was the one being punished and imprisoned. I was the one considered a threat and an embarrassment. I tried to go back to campus the following semester, but with my assailant still there and no support from the school, it was impossible for me to continue. In the end, I left and the school provided safe harbor for the rapist.

The following year, I transferred to another university far away, hoping to get a fresh start. But I could never forget what had been done to me, nor did I want to. I was and I still am determined to improve accountability, to change laws, policies, and protocols so that no one will have to go through what I went through. I learned of a peer group called Sexual Health Awareness & Rape Education (SHARE), in which students undergo a semester of training to educate others on sexual assault and risk-reduction. This was exactly what I needed to get involved in. I was tired of feeling badly for myself and was ready to use my experience to help others.

Being a SHARE peer was the most empowering experience of my life. It allowed me to educate myself as well as others and to make new friends who were also dedicated to the cause. Facilitating workshops was the most difficult part of my healing process. At each workshop, students—both male and female—consistently blamed women for sexual assaults. Students blamed the woman for what she was wearing or for how much she drank, implying that she was "asking for it." They criticized her for saying "NO" only five times instead of twenty. If she didn't really "want it," they wondered, why didn't she scream or hurt him? I often heard "What do women expect? They shouldn't go out and drink in the first place" and "It's not really rape because she brought him back to her room and she was flirting with him all night."

As part of the workshop, the class read a sexual assault scenario that had actually occurred on campus, a scenario very similar to my own experience. After students read it, I asked how many people thought that the woman had been raped. Generally, in a class of thirty people, no more than five raised their hands. I wanted to scream or cry, out of hurt and frustration, and sometimes I did. I used all my powers of persuasion in that short time to challenge students to examine their own beliefs about sexual assault. It was clear that some students were never going to change how they felt, but there were others who came to me after class to thank me for teaching them things about rape that they'd never really known. Often, students shared with me their own experiences of sexual assault. My teaching and advocacy were not limited to SHARE workshops. I reinforced these issues at every opportunity to friends and acquaintances.

Our society knows little to nothing about what sexual assault is. Many people do not know the definitions of assault, and very few know what to do when faced with an assault or rape crisis. Furthermore, people who are knowledgeable about these issues do not have much support in this country. I now work at the college I transferred to, as the Program Director for Sexual Assault and Relationship Violence at the Office for Sexual Health & Violence Prevention. People often say, "That's great, how noble of you." But in the same breath, they try to tell me that sexual assault "will never go away," that it is "just how men are." Students and adults still often label as "slutty" all women who say they were raped, believing that women claim rape when they regret having sex. Many sympathize with the "innocent" guy who must endure the reputation of being a rapist. I rarely encounter people who believe the woman. When I tell people that one woman in four will be a victim of rape or attempted rape by the time she graduates college, I get laughed at as if I'd told a funny joke. Yet it is my privilege to educate people about sexual assault, to tell my story, and to show other women that there are people who will believe and support us, that we all can be survivors.

Each day, when I tell my story, I wish more than anything that I could conclude by saying that my attacker is now in jail or that he has sought help and is no longer a danger to any of us. Instead, I finish by saying that he was never given an appropriate sanction for the acts he committed against me.

I believe that raising awareness, showing support, and educating others will lead to fewer sexual assaults, and I believe such efforts will give women the strength and encouragement they need to report their assaults. Ultimately, this will lead to more convictions, as potential jurors are freed from the myths that have prevailed in our society. I now know what I want people in this world to learn from me: that I will not let anyone blame me or punish me for being a victim, that I remained strong even when it seemed hopeless, and I never doubted what I knew to be the truth.

ANGELA

When I broke up with my high school sweetheart of four years, I actually felt liberated. The relationship had not been a healthy one. I had endured years of verbal and emotional abuse that left my self-esteem in ruins. I had spent most of those years worrying about losing "the love of my life," when I should have been worrying about losing myself. Regardless, I had found the strength to move on and was focused on making the most of my fresh start.

I began to spend more time with friends I had neglected for far too long and I started to feel like my old self again. I was a sophomore in college, studying nursing, and I was finally able to enjoy life as an adult. I took more care with my appearance, I exercised several times a week, wore makeup, and bought some new clothes. I made a conscious decision to love myself and I was getting better at it every day.

Thanksgiving break came, and I went home to celebrate with my family. That weekend, I was invited to a party at the home of an old friend. It was quite exciting because on more than one occasion, I had hoped to become more than just friends with him. I decided that

Saturday would be the perfect time to see if there was still chemistry between us. I put on some jeans and my cutest button-down shirt and went to the party.

I was happy to see an old girlfriend there. We hugged as if we hadn't seen each other in decades. The host of the party greeted me with a bear hug and a kiss on the cheek. I knew I was blushing, but I didn't care. Later, in the kitchen, he was teasing my girlfriend. She wanted a quarter and he told her, "If you want it, come and get it." He put the quarter in his mouth. She tried to pry open his lips with her fingers but it wasn't working. I sauntered over and said, "I'll get it." I planted a big kiss on his mouth and retrieved the coin. He smiled and so did I. Apparently, the chemistry was still there.

I didn't know it at the time, but my friend was fuming. Apparently, she also had a crush on this guy and was jealous that I was getting in the way. Shortly after I kissed him, we ran out of beer and my friend and I were sent to get some more. She worked at a local gas station and we knew we could buy alcohol there even though we weren't of legal drinking age. At the gas station, we bought the beer with no trouble at all and stayed to talk with her coworkers for a few minutes. The two men who worked there were older than us by about seven years. One of the men seemed to be eyeing me, but I shrugged it off until he said to me in his native Boston accent, "You have the most beautiful blue eyes I have ever seen." My jaw dropped. This mature and amazing-looking man had given me a compliment and I was flattered. My companion seemed to sense his interest in me and she invited both of the guys back to the party. One of the guys stayed to finish his shift, but the one who seemed interested in me returned with us. My friend whispered to me that I should "go for it." I was pretty inebriated by then, and starting to think she was right.

When we got back to the party, most of the people had gone home. The host of the party had passed out in his bedroom and it seemed we were too late with the beer. My girlfriend left to drive some people home and I worried about driving home myself. She suggested that I get a ride from her coworker who had joined us for the evening. After all, he hadn't had anything to drink that night. I was nervous because I had just met him, but I decided to let him drive me home.

"It's a bummer that all your friends took off," he said.

"I know. I'm not even tired yet," I replied.

"We could go to my apartment for a little while to watch a movie or something. What do you think?" He sensed my hesitation. "Come on, I don't bite!"

I finally agreed to go to his apartment for a little while. I sat down on the couch in the living room while he popped in a movie and cracked open a couple of beers. Knowing that I had already had too much to drink, I didn't drink anymore. He seemed to know all of the lines to the movie and tried to impress me by reciting them. About halfway through the movie, he leaned in and gave me a lingering kiss. My body tingled and I snuggled up next to him so he could put his arm around me while we watched.

By the time the movie was over, I felt sober again and thought it was time for me to leave. He said he didn't want me to go yet and wondered if I would dance with him. He turned on some slow dancing music and led me by the hand to the middle of his living room. We kissed again and he rubbed my back while we danced. I was nervous but excited. Then he started to unbutton my shirt. I pulled away but he pulled me back, a little more forcefully than I was comfortable with. I was torn. I wanted to leave, but I didn't want to mess things up with this newfound love interest. We had gotten along great up until that point. He began to kiss my neck, then tried again to unbutton my shirt. This time I tried to push him away, but he ripped open my shirt and tripped me, sending me falling onto the carpet. I was alarmed at how aggressive he'd become and I began to feel scared. He said, "Come on, I can tell you like me." He held me down with his forearm across my neck, leaving his other hand free to undress himself and me. I kept telling him to let me go, but he wouldn't. He just kept saying over and over again, "Trust me, you'll love it." My body froze and my mind felt numb.

After what seemed like forever, he got up and said in a threatening tone, "Stay right there." Naked, he walked up the stairs to his bedroom. I immediately got up, threw on my clothes as best I could and searched for my car keys. I finally found them behind the toaster in the kitchen where he had hidden them. I ran out the door to my car. As I started my vehicle, I saw him peering through his window. I sped off and began to sob.

I couldn't go home. What would I tell my parents? I didn't even understand what had just happened. I decided to drive back over to my friend's house where the party had been. His parents were gone and I figured I could crash there. As I walked into his house, I saw that my girlfriend was asleep on the couch. I decided not to wake her. I went downstairs and found my friend who lived there. In a voice that was not quite awake, he asked, "Did you bring the beer?" I started to cry and he woke up. He asked me several times what was wrong, but all I could do was cry. Finally, I told him the whole story. He was infuriated and said that he should just go get his gun and "shoot the bastard." I was shaken and scared. Finally, I felt calm enough to rest. He got me some blankets and offered to let me sleep on his spare bed.

The next morning, I was surprised but relieved to see that my friend had already left. I didn't know how to tell her about what her coworker had done to me. I found out later that she already knew that he had been investigated for similar offenses in the past. It took me years to forgive her for that.

The host of the party was sober now and he went home with me to talk to my parents. They were shocked and angry but fully supportive of me. After telling them what happened, I decided to take a long, hot shower. I knew nothing of rape exams or DNA evidence. I wasn't even sure I wanted to report it to the police anyway. After all, I had been drinking and had gone to the home of someone I had just met late at night. I had even let him kiss me and enjoyed it. Some of the blame had to be mine, right? I thought so.

Later that day, the man who had raped me called me. I wasn't prepared for that. He actually wanted to meet me after work that night. I didn't say much to him. I didn't tell him that I would meet him, and got off the phone as quickly as possible. I couldn't believe that he had called and acted as if nothing was wrong. I told my parents about the phone call and they were furious.

A few days later, I finally felt ready to report the assault to the police. A friend of mine accompanied me to the police station. He believed me and told me it wasn't my fault. It's funny how much of a difference one person's words can make. Those words made me feel that I would be able to make it through my ordeal. After telling my story to the police, I learned that the perpetrator had been investigated for several similar incidents, but had never formally been charged. Although I knew it would be the beginning of a long and difficult process, I decided to proceed with charges.

Weeks passed and I heard nothing. Finally, a letter came from the county attorney. It stated that while she believed that my story was true, there was not enough evidence to move forward with the prosecution. I was devastated. Why wasn't my word good enough? I felt like I had gone through all that embarrassment and heartache for nothing.

I had no idea what to do next. I returned to school, but I asked for an extension on my assignments and postponed my final exams. I wanted to take a semester off, but was informed by the school that time off would jeopardize my scholarship. I tried to appeal this policy, but the school was unwilling to make an exception regardless of my reason, so I went back to my hometown.

I decided to take a little time for myself to reflect, to mourn, and to heal. I spent a lot of time alone. I tried seeing a therapist, but it didn't quite work for me. I knew that if I were ever going to heal, I would have to figure out on my own how to be whole again. I decided that

I had two choices. I could be a victim or I could be a survivor. I knew that I couldn't change what had happened to me, only how I would deal with it. Before long, I enrolled at a local liberal arts university and changed my major to sociology. The more I studied, the more I felt I was destined for a career that would allow me to help people. I was able to work through my feelings about being sexually assaulted and was even able to share my experience with other survivors. My friends stopped tiptoeing around me and I began to feel as though my life was finally getting back on track.

I still thought about the assault, but it no longer consumed my thoughts. I even tried getting involved in a few romantic relationships again, but it was difficult for me to trust or be intimate with anyone. When a relationship started to get serious, I would run or find a way to sabotage the relationship. While everything else in my life seemed to be going well, I was unable to make a relationship with a man work and that was extremely frustrating. Eventually, I came to realize that the problem was probably not with the men I was seeing; it was my problem. I did a lot of reading on healthy relationships, spent time with male friends and tried to convince myself that not all men are perpetrators.

Then one day I met a man who made me feel alive again. He listened to me like no one else had and, for the first time, I was able to imagine a future that would include another person. There was something about him that I felt I could trust. We weren't together very long before I shared my story with him. After we had dated for a couple of years, we were married.

I finally finished school. I advanced in my career and although I was feeling successful, I still felt as though something was missing from my life. I did not feel fulfilled. One day, there was an ad in the paper calling for applicants for a position at our local crime victim service agency. The position was titled Education and Outreach Coordinator and it instantly appealed to me. I wasn't sure if it would pay as much as I was earning at my current job, but I didn't care. I knew that I had to apply.

As soon as I walked in the door for my interview, I felt at home. The people in the office were welcoming, and as they spoke to me about their mission and their role in helping victims, I knew that I wanted to work in victims' services. I was offered the position and accepted it.

As I worked with crime victims, I gained knowledge in many areas including how to recognize healthy relationships. The more I spoke with young people about their relationships, the more I realized that my marriage was not a healthy one. While my husband and I had three children together and appeared to have a happy marriage, I was uneasy about some of the dynamics of the relationship. I loved my husband, but instead of getting easier, being intimate with him was getting more difficult each time. We argued about it almost every day. I couldn't just give in and he couldn't understand. I thought I had married the man who I'd spend the rest of my life with, but it didn't last. We divorced and are working together to co-parent our children. Although extremely difficult, our divorce was the best thing for everyone involved.

Deciding to work with victims of crime has been one of the best decisions that I have ever made. Not only have I been able to reevaluate the direction my life is going, I have also been able to continue my never-ending healing process. I have been able to help others who have gone through similar experiences to navigate their way through the legal system and to find their own courage to heal. Even though my assailant was never prosecuted, I have found tremendous satisfaction in supporting victims and in making sure their perpetrators are held accountable.

But I have to say that my favorite part of the work that I do is prevention. I have been able to talk to children as young as three years old, as well as to high school and college students, about how to prevent sexual abuse and assault. I know the statistics; when I speak in classrooms or lecture halls, I am aware that several of the people in the audience have been or will be sexually assaulted. For this reason, I am compelled to do the best job that I can. Everyone wishes that sexual victimization would end, but I wish for more than that. I wish to save lives—the lives of potential victims as well as potential perpetrators. If I have prevented even one person from becoming a victim or a perpetrator, then all of the work that I have done has been worthwhile. I no longer regret the pain that I endured as a result of being sexually assaulted. I believe that my life is exactly as it should be. My mother always told me that what doesn't kill us makes us stronger. She was right.

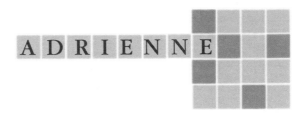

ADRIENNE

Journal Entry   October 22, 2001
Letter to the Perpetrators

Who do you think you are??? You don't even know me!! What made you think you could just take me away? You stole me from the party, from my friends. Where did you take me? What did you do to me? Was it all three of you? Did you take turns? Was it fun for you?

I was nineteen years old and at a party with some friends from work. We were having a great time, drinking and socializing. I remember dancing on the lawn. Then suddenly, I was in the back seat of a car with three strange men I didn't know. What was happening? Who were these people? Where were they taking me?

I panicked. Something wasn't right. I looked for a way out, but the car had only two doors. I could not jump out. I knew my life was in jeopardy. Although I couldn't remember what had happened beforehand, I knew I needed to get control of what was going to happen next. That's when I began to beg and plead, but to no avail. They did whatever they wanted to me. I felt like a zombie. Why couldn't I think straight? Why couldn't I react? What they were doing was wrong, but I couldn't move, couldn't control it. My body was defenseless. I surrendered to them, giving them my body in hopes of living to see another day.

My strategy worked. I lived. I try not to question why.

I had been drugged and sexually assaulted. After the attack, the three rapists brought me home. Ironically, the same people who violated me, took away my innocence and shattered my world were the people who brought me to safety. Finally at home, I thought, "At least it's all over." Little did I know, it had just begun.

Journal Entry (continued)   October 22, 2001

How could you do it? How could you violate me and take away my innocence? Did you think I would not wake up? Were you prepared? Did you plan the evening out? Why did you take me home? Were you scared? Where is my shoe? Why was I muddy, why was I wet? Was it hard to get my underwear down, so hard that you just didn't bother to pull it back up?

Do you think about it everyday? Do you replay it in your head over and over? Because I do. Does it invade your dreams? Do you realize you've screwed up my whole life, every aspect of it? You have no heart, no soul, no conscience. I'm so angry! I'm so mad! I wish you were dead! I want you to die a long and gruesome death. You've tainted me; you stole my innocence without my even knowing. Did you think I would not remember?

So many unanswered questions . . . it's so hard to get closure. You've taken over my life—you haunt me! But you're not going to win. I am strong and I will beat you! I hate you with every breath I take, but that doesn't bother me because at least I am breathing. You may have violated me and taken away something special from me, but you can't take away my life. I know justice will be served, if not in this life, then in the afterlife.

The world is a cruel, harsh place. One learns this lesson after a personal invasion. That's what rape is. Rape is often compared to death, but I think of it as robbery because something so personal, so special is taken from you. What is frustrating, though, is that at first, you cannot quite pinpoint what's been taken. But before long, you notice what is missing: dignity, pride, innocence, strength, courage, hope, love, trust, kindness, warmth, beauty, belonging, direction. These gifts you once treasured—they're gone now. And the hard part is accepting that and beginning to move on.

Who was I before this happened, before I was raped of my innocence, my trust, my spirit? It's painful to recall how innocent and fun-loving I was. That night, parts of me died—my optimism, my love for life, my thirst for adventure. Sometimes it seems pointless to acknowledge who I was before the assault because I am not the same person anymore. How do I deal with this loss? How do I deal with what has happened? There is no set method, each individual reacts differently and must discover his or her own path. For me, that path has led to some amazing accomplishments as well as some horrifying realizations. The key is to take it one step at a time.

Soon after my assault, I became very vocal. I thought about that horrible night every second of every day. I had this awful pain and didn't know how to relieve it. I figured if I were going to have to live with it and be uncomfortable, everyone around me was going to live with it too. Initially, I spoke out because I was mad at the world. Eventually, I realized it was necessary to speak out not only for myself but for others as well. Sexual assault is one of those topics no one ever brings up because it makes people feel so uncomfortable. Since most people don't realize the effects of sexual assault, I took it upon myself to let people know what had happened to me and how I felt. This was the beginning of my recovery.

At first I wanted to separate my assault from my life, but I realized that it couldn't be—it is now a part of me. So I sought help. Counseling, and speaking with a victim advocate got me started in the right direction. I attended a support group where I found it extremely helpful to meet women who have been through similar experiences. We helped each other by sharing our stories. The most important part of surviving and recovery is developing a support system. We're living in an awesome time right now. Not too long ago, we couldn't even talk about rape. It was considered shameful, something to be kept secret. However, now we're fortunate that victims of crime are encouraged to speak out. There are so many opportunities and ways to get help, but you have to ask. Unfortunately, this is probably one of the most difficult things to do. However, once you take the initial step, there will be people willing to help, and they'll support you the whole way. I know that I can't go through this alone and I can't emphasize enough that without the people from whom I've sought help, I wouldn't be here today. My support team has given me the strength to succeed.

Writing has been a very important part of my recovery process. Journaling gives me an opportunity to voice my thoughts and emotions. It is an outlet that helps me to solve problems and relieve frustration. Writing allows me to track my recovery process. I can look at previous entries in my journal and see how far I've come. These early entries also help me to remember. As time passes, I begin to forget. Forgetting might sound like healing, but it's not. I need to be able to acknowledge what has happened in the past in order to make sense of today.

Anniversaries are important too. Not only the big ones, like one year or two years after my rape. At first, I acknowledged the 4th and 5th day of each month as an anniversary. As my rape became a more distant part of my past, the small anniversaries became less important, but I still took note of them. Anniversaries are a time to mourn, to remember, or to do something good for myself. Sometimes they're a celebration of life. Always, they're a time for reflection. Regardless, these days are mine and I allow myself to do what I want with them.

Journal Entry   **February 3, 2003**

Why is it that the further away it gets, the more difficult the anniversaries become? I feel like it's a constant struggle. Well, it's been a year and a half—a whole year and a half since that night, the night that changed me forever. The night when three men stripped me of my dignity. What a horrible violation it was. A rape, not only of my body, but of my mind and soul as well. I lost everything that night, everything that mattered.

And now, it's just a memory. I thought I'd never forget the horror and pain I felt that night. I swore to myself I'd always remember the anger and hatred I felt. But now, I don't under-stand why I can't physically feel those emotions anymore. As time lapses, that night is becoming only a vague memory, a little tiny experience I keep in a special place in my mind, I thought I'd be able to take it out whenever I wanted to, and feel—physically feel—the pain again. But it's so hard now— I try to and it's so hard. Is it wrong of me to be upset that I've forgotten it? It's become so much a part of my life, so much a part of who I am, that I'm afraid to let it go. It is who I am, in a sick sort of way; it's my security blanket, the one thing that sets me apart from everyone else.

And now, well, now it's fading away, it's slipping so fast. Soon it will have been two years, then three, then ten, and soon it will be like it never happened. And I don't want it to be like that. I never want to forget it. I just can't let it go. And I'm so mad that I can no longer feel it.

Why has it become so easy to forget? I feel like I've been raped again, raped of my memory, and I'm angry. I can't accept the fact that I might be ready to move on, that I might be ready to let it go. Instead of embracing this wonderful accomplishment in my recovery process, I am angry and upset with myself for arriving at this point. I feel like I've betrayed myself.

Why can't I accept it and come to peace with things?

While it's difficult to let go of the past, it's sometimes just as difficult to build for the future. I continue to struggle when interacting with men. New issues always arise. I hate addressing these issues, but I realize that something must be done so I can continue to evolve, to grow within my recovery process. I need help and guidance. I know that I am a wonderful person with many great qualities, but love just takes time.

Journal Entry   March 9, 2004

I think one of the hardest parts in recovery is the point where you have begun to forgive the opposite sex, where you have begun to acknowledge that you need someone to offer you love, trust, and support; however, no one is to be found. It's somewhat devastating. I know I don't need a man to be complete, but it would be nice to have someone to share myself with. Yeah, I have girlfriends, real good and loving friends, but sometimes it's not enough to fill that "void" in your life. Sometimes I feel so empty and alone. I have so much to offer, but there's no one there to receive it.

People say, "You'll find someone, just give it time. It will happen when you least expect it." I'll believe it when I see it. I don't think I'll ever find someone.

First of all, who would want and accept someone with all the baggage I have? Rape equals issues. Before the rape, I was a virgin by choice. I am still a virgin, but for different reasons. When you see how sex can be used as a brutal weapon—how it can hurt someone so badly and take away so much—you begin to take sex so much more seriously. Plus, sex has become somewhat scary. Sexual acts can trigger unwanted memories.

Which brings me to baggage item number two: my rape may disgust some men. It's never someone's fault for being assaulted, but the thought that someone has taken advantage of their girl could be a turn-off for some guys. And then there is the emotional roller coaster my life has become. Since the assault, I have had massive mood swings that are unpredictable, even to me.

In addition to all that, I have major trust issues. If, by the good grace of God, I even find someone I can connect with, who's to say I'll let myself trust him? I'm so afraid of being hurt. Yet, by remaining alone, I feel like I am constantly hurting myself.

Maybe a man won't fill my "void" and make things better, but, I've tried everything else. I've gotten all the help I possibly can. And now I'm stuck in this rut. I'm so lonely and depressed. And I wonder, if a relationship with a decent guy won't help, what will? I'm scared to find out. I feel lost. I need someone to hold me and let me know it will be all right.

What if I always feel this way? Will I ever be complete?

Each person deals with recovery in a different way. Getting involved has helped me. Through volunteer work, I found opportunities to help others. I have served as a peer educator, speaking on my campus and in my community about sexual assault, alcohol, and sexual health. Recently, I have reached a milestone in my own sexual assault recovery process; I have always been pretty open when it comes to talking about my rape, but I am now putting my name and face with my story for all to see. I believe this shows that this horrid crime is very real and can reach us all.

In my public outreach, I have written articles and spoken to audiences about my own experience with rape, how it has affected my life, and how I've turned a horrible event into a positive experience by giving back to the community. The first time I spoke to a group of people about my rape and recovery process, I was exhilarated. I was amazed that people were truly listening to me and were concerned with what I had to say. I was able to capture the attention of an audience and educate people about sexual assault and the effects it has on an individual.

Although sharing my story helps me with my own recovery process, what keeps me going is thinking about how many women and men I've touched, how many have been given a voice through my own story. Since my first talk, I've spoken to many audiences, some with as few as eight people and some that have numbered in the hundreds. Regardless of the size of the audience or the type of event, I know I am raising awareness about the crime of sexual assault. Whatever else happens, I know I want to continue my public speaking, to reach out to others and also to see where it might take me.

It's incredible that a single event can change your whole life—change who you are and your perspective on life. I never would have believed that recovering from rape would be so difficult. But it has been. I hate the fact that I was raped. It haunts my existence, it is always there, but I can't change the past and I am proud that I have made the best of a bad situation by not letting it control my life. My rape added another dimension to my existence, but it is has not replaced all the others, it does not define who I am. I want people to know that I am a regular young woman with a normal life and great expectations.

I would never wish rape or crime upon anyone. However, I now know that survival and recovery can be a positive experience. I am extremely lucky. Thanks to my amazing family and friends, I haven't had to face things all alone. Some days are good and some are bad, but I am grateful for each day that I'm alive. I know that my rape will never go away, and I understand that at times I may feel weak, but I also know that as long as I continue to receive support and understanding I will continue to grow and become an even stronger person.

I've come far in my recovery process, but I have also come to realize that, ultimately, there is no "recovery" from a rape. It's not like the flu—it won't just go away. However, I do know I am and will continue to be a survivor. I will continue with my activism; I will strive to help end violence against women. If it weren't for the assault, I may never have become involved in such a worthy cause. Educating people and raising awareness about sexual assault is now an important part of my life and recovery process. It empowers me, allows me to be true to myself, and gives my life meaning. Through family and friends I have been reassured that I am still me—an honor student, a social butterfly, athletic, and funny. But, I have also been deeply changed, strengthened in some ways, more certain in my beliefs and values. I no longer minimize my experience in order to make others feel comfortable. The gruesome reality needs to be known. Women need to share their stories in order to help end violence against women.

Journal Entry   **August 1, 2004**

I'm amazed at how far I've come, but at the same time, I'm overwhelmed by how far I still have to go. In a few short days, it will be the three-year anniversary of my rape. Three years of love, life, and laughter, as well as three years of pain, anger, and frustration. I have learned and grown so much in such a short time. And it has all stemmed from that one horrible event, which altered my world forever.

I'm no longer upset when I think about it. I don't think "what if" anymore. I don't wonder what my life might be like had I never been assaulted. I've come to the realization that, although you can't change the past, you can shape the future.

I now know why this happened to me. Not as punishment, not to make me suffer. But to help me help others. With my voice, my words, my courage, and my commitment, I am able to spread the word about sexual assault and can be a voice for others. I truly believe I've made a difference in this world and will continue to make a difference in the future. I am no longer afraid of what the future holds. I know that I have the strength to handle everything that comes my way. There is still so much more for me to learn and so much for me to share. I am eager and excited to face the future head-on.

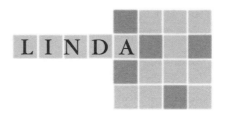

LINDA

In the summer of 1981, I was on top of the world. I had graduated from college a few years before and moved back to my hometown in Virginia. After sharing dorm rooms and apartments all through college, I was thrilled to have my very own apartment, which I had carefully decorated to suit my taste. I had a great job, plenty of friends, and an active social life. That summer, the future seemed wide open and full of possibilities.

Like most other August evenings, the day had been unbearably hot and the night didn't bring much relief. My apartment had no air conditioning, so I kept all the windows open and used a large fan to circulate air in the bedroom. Even with the fan, it was too hot to sleep that night, so after watching a preseason football game on TV, I stayed up to watch a late movie. Finally, around 2:00 a.m., I made my way to bed.

I was restless in the stifling heat so it didn't surprise me too much when I awoke to find my clock radio unplugged. Thinking I had flung out an arm in my sleep and accidentally dislodged the plug, I plugged the clock in again and went back to sleep. Oddly, I awoke a second time to an unplugged clock, fixed it, and rolled over. Then it happened again and I began to feel uneasy. When I woke up a fourth time to see a man standing over my bed, I was overcome by terror.

I tried to scream but no sound emerged. The man put a cold metal object to my throat and told me not to make any noise. The fog of sleep lifted and I knew without a doubt that my life was in danger. The man put a pillow over my face and proceeded to rape me over the course of what seemed like hours. Because I couldn't see him, I strained to recognize the assailant by his voice. He spoke very little and my heart sank when I realized his voice was not familiar to me.

At some point during the assault, I began to focus on doing whatever I could to get out of it alive. The rapist asked me a few questions and I answered them calmly and truthfully. I didn't want to risk angering him enough to kill me. When he told me he was leaving and not to move for ten minutes. I followed his instructions. The man's warning turned out to be unnecessary, though, for I found my body just as paralyzed as my voice had been when he had first appeared in my room.

When daylight arrived, I made myself get out of bed. Instinctively, I grabbed a steak knife from the kitchen, got in my car, and drove to the hospital. On the way, I passed a police officer sitting in his car in a grocery store parking lot. I told him what had happened and he followed me to the emergency room. The experience of having evidence collected from my body at the hospital was not pleasant, but I was lucky to be treated by a young resident who was very gentle and compassionate. The doctor and nurse collected the evidence and handed it over to the police. Years later, I would be glad I had gone through that difficult exam.

The police combed my apartment for clues but found little. In 1981, there was no such thing as DNA evidence and no way to collect much more than hair samples and fingerprints. The forensic evidence yielded very little—just a blood type from the semen on the bed sheets with no one to match it to and a shoeprint from where the rapist had hidden in my shower. The police asked me for the names of every man with whom I'd had contact in the past month. They interviewed them all and even took shoes from each one of them, but nothing matched. The detectives took me to a police hypnotist, hoping that I had seen more than I remembered and that hypnosis would help me to recall more details, but that didn't work either. After a few months, the investigators called less and less often until we gradually lost contact and my case went cold.

I call the next part of my life the "in-between time." For sixteen years, I lived in a very lonely place, feeling cut off from all that had made my life fulfilling in the past. At first, I was afraid to go out of the house and when I did, I found myself looking at every man in the grocery store or across from me at a red light. Was he the one? Was it a colleague, a neighbor, someone who went to my church? Was he following me? Was he going to make good on his promise to come back and kill me because I had gone to the police?

For a long time, I found it hard to trust anyone but my family and closest friends. The life that had seemed full of possibilities was suddenly reduced to two crucial priorities—feeling safe again and being able to function in a world that now felt hostile and dangerous. During the first year after the rape, a gifted counselor helped me to find the courage to venture back into the world, to enroll in graduate school and to begin to set goals for my life, but when she suggested it was time to talk about the possibility of dating again, I decided our work together was finished. I felt certain my dating days were over. How could I ever be interested in a man when all men were suspect?

As I began to function better outwardly, friends and family stopped asking questions about the rape and how I was coping. I'm sure it seemed that I was doing just fine, but inside I felt isolated and alone. The rape became my constant companion—like a heavy pack that was invisible to others but that was always there for me to carry. I think those who love me were relieved to see me getting "better," but I knew I was not getting better, just handling my pain differently. I knew it wasn't just going to go away.

I managed to accomplish a lot during those in-between years. I finished graduate school and then taught at a nearby university for a couple of years. At age 30, I followed a call to ordained ministry and went to a seminary in South Carolina. Following graduation and ordination, I served as a parish pastor, campus minister, and seminary development officer. Though I knew that my experience as a rape survivor made me more compassionate toward others in crisis and made me a better pastor, I rarely spoke about the rape. I was living two different lives—outwardly competent and successful, inwardly broken and lonely. It would take a while, but soon those two lives would be brought together in a most amazing way.

In July 1997, I was working as a development officer at a seminary in South Carolina. For no reason that I can explain, I picked up the phone one afternoon and called the police department of the town where I had been raped. I couldn't remember the names of the detectives who had worked on my case, but I was hoping someone could give me some information that would allow me to gain a sense of closure on the rape. It felt like a long shot and I was pretty sure no one would remember me. About an hour later, I received a call back from Lieutenant Don Weaver, the investigator who had handled my case sixteen years earlier. Not only did he remember me, but he had been trying to get in touch with me because he wanted to reopen my case and see what he could find out before he retired in a few years. I was stunned, elated, and scared. What if the case was reopened and we learned no more than we already knew? But I decided that this opportunity was a rare gift and that I had to pursue it as far as I could.

The police found the original physical evidence from my case in their evidence room where it had sat, untouched, for all those years. Inside the sealed cardboard box was the evidence from the hospital along with about a dozen orphaned left sneakers. The linens from my bed were preserved inside a big garbage bag. Lieutenant Weaver brought the evidence to the state forensic lab in Richmond, where he requested a forensic scientist named Lisa Scheirmeier to process the materials. So much had changed in forensic science since 1981—now there was DNA analysis. I often joke that I was lucky to have been raped in Virginia, but when it comes to forensic science it's true. Virginia's labs and scientists are among the best in the country.

That doesn't mean the case went smoothly. Even though Scheirmeier was the best person to handle the evidence, she had more than enough to do with her current caseload. Prompted by my never-ending phone calls, Lieutenant Weaver and Lisa made numerous requests until Lisa's boss finally gave her permission to do the DNA analysis. Although the evidence had been sealed for sixteen years, it was somewhat degraded and fragile, and there wasn't very much of it. After using up almost all the evidence, Scheirmeier decided to wait until the lab installed brand-new state of the art equipment before she ran some final tests.

In the meantime, my life underwent many changes. The reopened case gave me the chance to talk with my family and friends again about the rape. We shared feelings we hadn't been able to share sixteen years earlier, which was a wonderfully healing experience. I told other people about what was happening and asked for their support. To my surprise, I got it. I had always feared that if I told people about the rape, they would be repulsed and turn away. Maybe some people did, but I didn't notice. What I found instead were others who had gone through experiences like mine and who had never talked about them either, and I encountered people who wanted to help but just needed to be asked.

In the fall of 1998, the bishop of my denomination in Virginia asked if I would become the interim pastor for a congregation whose pastor had just left because of sexual misconduct. Never one to turn down a challenge, I accepted. Once I was settled back in Virginia, I resumed my wait for forensic results. It took two years of touch-and-go forensic work, but finally, in 1999, Scheirmeier solved the mystery. She had gathered enough DNA data to form a profile of the man who had raped me. When the evidence ruled out the police's primary suspect, Lisa decided to run the profile through Virginia's database of convicted felons and got what is known as a "cold hit." The perpetrator turned out to be a convicted serial rapist who had been arrested three years after my rape and sentenced to several life sentences for raping three other women. I don't think I ever met him, though he lived just down the street from me when the rape occurred.

I was ready to go all the way now, to push for prosecution and conviction of the rapist so I could finally get the closure I'd sought for so many years. The police, forensic personnel, and I were excited about the next step, but we were cut short by a prosecutor who refused to take the case, despite the DNA evidence and a confession.

I have struggled for several years with the anger and disappointment this decision caused, but it does not diminish all that I've gained from my remarkable second chance.

Because my case was so old, had been solved by DNA analysis, and involved a cold hit, it got a lot of media attention. I agreed to do interviews for a national magazine and some TV news programs. My case was unusual and I knew I had a unique chance to use the voice I had once lost to raise public awareness of sexual assault and its survivors, maybe even to speak for someone who didn't yet have her voice back. The publicity pushed me to disclose my experience to the congregation I was serving. It was then that I understood the depth of their compassion and support. I'm still amazed that we were able to travel the same road to healing together. A congregation dealing with the aftermath of clergy sexual misconduct faces some of the same issues as survivors of sexual assault, including abuse of power, betrayal of trust, shame, and shattered faith. The first tentative step the congregation and I took together was to begin to speak openly about what had happened to us and to acknowledge our anger and grief. That sharing was crucial in building our trust in one another and in God.

My first public speaking opportunity came in 2001 when the bill calling for reauthorization of the Violence Against Women Act was stalled in Congress. This important legislation provides funds for education and advocacy about sexual and domestic violence. I was invited to speak at a congressional press conference designed to influence legislators to pass the bill. Imagine my amazement when I rose to speak and turned to see a dozen powerful lawmakers standing behind me! That day was a turning point for me. I discovered that the story I had kept locked inside for so long had a certain power. I decided not to keep silent any longer, but to tell my story to all who would listen. I have found healing in the process, for every time I tell my story, it loses a little bit of its hold on me. In addition, I hope that my sharing moves others to care about survivors of sexual assault.

In a couple of years, my life will be divided right down the middle—twenty-five years before the rape and twenty-five years after. The two halves of my life are very different. Before the rape, I didn't know much about the evil that exists in our world, but then I met it face-to-face. Since then, I have learned that because I survived the rape, I can get through most of what life throws at me. I have discovered a passion for reaching out to others who have been touched by evil, especially survivors of sexual and domestic violence. In *A Farewell to Arms*, Ernest Hemingway wrote, "The world breaks everyone, and afterward many are strong at the broken places." I know that by the grace of God, those words are true for me. Not one of us leaves this life untouched; I believe we all can be agents of healing to help others find the strength that only comes from surviving brokenness.

I still live with the burden of rape every day, only now the pack isn't quite so heavy and it isn't invisible anymore. I have some of the symptoms of post-traumatic stress syndrome and probably always will. I still struggle with dating relationships, but I was always pretty picky and have found other single women my age who share the same struggle. I find myself spending less time wondering what my life would have been like if I hadn't been raped and more time looking forward with excitement to what lies ahead. I have been blessed with loved ones who have stuck with me through some very tough times, with law enforcement and forensic professionals who are my heroes, and with many opportunities for healing along the way.

My life has followed many twists and turns, and at long last I can honestly say again that life is good. I am now pursuing a career in jewelry design, something I couldn't have imagined myself doing even a few years ago. One of the wonderful insights I have received as a part of my healing is that I have a creative side that brings me much joy. I use all kinds of beads and stones in my work but my favorite jewelry-making material is beach glass. Beach glass begins as discarded broken jars and bottles. These jagged bits and pieces wash out to sea and then end up on the beach amidst the shells and rocks. Years of being tumbled in the waves and blasted by sand and water turn sharp-edged bits of ordinary glass into treasures whose rough edges are worn completely smooth. It's easy to pass over beach glass, but when you sift through the sand and shells on the beach, you find it— brown and green and white and blue, each a gem, each unique in size and shape. I was surprised to learn that it can take fifteen or twenty years to completely smooth a piece of glass; that fact is kind of reassuring when I look back on how long God has been polishing me. Whenever I use a piece of beach glass in my jewelry, I'm reminded of Hemingway's words and my hope for all survivors—that they are made strong in the broken places, that their rough edges be smoothed, and that they find a beauty and purpose they may never have imagined for themselves.

JOURNAL

JOURNAL

JOURNAL

YOU ARE MAKING A DIFFERENCE

Crisis centers, coalitions, and organizations throughout the world continue to need financial assistance from individuals and private organizations to support essential programs and initiatives.

By purchasing *Voices of Courage*, you have made a difference. All profits from the sale of this book will be donated to organizations that work to raise awareness, educate society, and support survivors of sexual assault. An Advisory Council has been established by The Date Safe Project to choose the organizations that will receive the profits from this book.

In addition to the contribution you have made in buying *Voices of Courage*, please consider providing financial and/or human resources to the organizations listed on the following pages. Your gift of time or money can help reduce occurrences of sexual assault and support survivors of this horrific crime.

THE DATE SAFE PROJECT

The Date Safe Project is committed to being a national leader in the mission to teach youth and adults that "asking first" makes all the difference in creating safer intimacy and in decreasing occurrences of sexual assault.

Changing the old message of "No Means No" to "Do You Ask?" ensures that requesting consent becomes a natural part of human intimacy. This unique approach shifts the focus of responsibility from the individual about to be touched or kissed, to the individual who seeks to make an intimate gesture or act. A better understanding of the consent relationship leads to healthier dating and to a greater awareness of the many issues surrounding human sexuality and sexual assault.

The Date Safe Project provides students, educators, schools, and communities with interactive keynote presentations, workshops, books, and other educational resources that are filled with fun exercises, thought-provoking lessons, emotionally touching stories, and easy-to-implement concepts. Parents are given simple methods for talking with their kids about the important, but often awkward, issues raised when dating. Open communication between couples, and between parents and kids, are key factors in promoting healthy relationships and reducing sexual assault.

Website: www.thedatesafeproject.org

RESOURCES

Rape, Abuse & Incest National Network (RAINN) is the nation's largest anti-sexual assault organization. RAINN operates the National Sexual Assault Hotline at 1.800.656.HOPE. RAINN carries out programs to prevent sexual assault, help victims, and ensure that rapists are brought to justice. RAINN uses its extensive entertainment industry and community-based connections to educate more than 120 million Americans each year about sexual assault.

Toll-Free Hotline: (800) 656-HOPE
Website: www.rainn.org

MaleSurvivor, the National Organization on Male Sexual Victimization, is committed to preventing, healing, and eliminating all forms of sexual victimization of boys and men through treatment, research, education, advocacy, and activism. The organization maintains a website that includes a wealth of information for survivors and professionals about male sexual victimization as well as a Discussion Board and live Chat Room where survivors can network and support one another, anonymously if they wish. MaleSurvivor also publishes a newsletter and sponsors periodic conferences and healing retreats.

Website: www.malesurvivor.org

AdvocateWeb is the largest internet resource dealing with sexual misconduct, exploitation and abuse of clients by mental health professionals, medical professionals, clergy, lawyers, educators, and law enforcement officials. AdvocateWeb offers extensive free resources for victims, survivors, their families, friends, victim advocates, and professionals seeking to address this problem.

Website: www.advocateweb.org

The Awareness Center is the Jewish Coalition Against Sexual Abuse/Assault (JCASA). JCASA is dedicated to addressing sexual violence in Jewish communities around the world.

Phone: (443) 857-5560
Website: www.theawarenesscenter.org

FaithTrust Institute is a national multifaith organization working to end sexual and domestic violence. We provide communities and advocates with the tools and knowledge they need to address the religious and cultural issues related to abuse. Through training, consultation, and educational materials, we equip religious leaders to address sexual and domestic violence in their communities.

Website: www.faithtrustinstitute.org

Men Can Stop Rape mobilizes male youth to prevent men's violence against women. The organization builds young men's capacity to challenge harmful aspects of traditional masculinity, to value alternative visions of male strength, and to embrace their vital role as allies with women and girls in fostering healthy relationships and gender equity.

Phone: (202) 265-6530
Website: www.mencanstoprape.org

National Sexual Violence Resource Center (NSVRC) is a comprehensive collection and distribution center for information, statistics, and resources related to sexual violence. It serves as a resource for coalitions, rape crisis centers, allied organizations, and others working to eliminate sexual assault. The NSVRC does not provide direct services to sexual assault victims but rather supports those who do.

Toll-Free: (877) 739-3895
Website: www.nsvrc.org

Security On Campus, Inc. (SOC) is the only national non-profit organization devoted exclusively to providing services to the victims of violence on college campuses and to educating students. When SOC works with victims, university policies are changed for the better.

Toll-Free: (888) 251-7959
Website: www.securityoncampus.org

Stop It Now! is a national non-profit organization working to prevent child sexual abuse using the tools of public health. Since 1992, its public policy, public education, and research programs have protected children by emphasizing adult and community responsibility.

Toll-Free: (888) PREVENT
Website: www.stopitnow.org

State Coalitions Against Sexual Assault & Local Rape Crisis Centers have been established throughout the country and can be found at:

Website: www.voicesofcourage.com/resources.

SUGGESTED READING

A listing of the following books, along with many more, may be found at: www.voicesofcourage.com/resources.

After the Silence: Rape and My Journey Back. Nancy Venable Raine (Three Rivers Press, 1999).

Allies in Healing: When the Person You Love was Sexually Abused as a Child. Laura Davis (NY: Harper Perennial, 1991).

The Courage to Heal Workbook—For Women and Men Survivors of Child Sexual Abuse. Laura Davis (NY: Harper Perennial; 1st edition, 1990).

The Date Rape Prevention Book: The Essential Guide For Girls And Women. Scott Lindquist (Sourcebooks Inc., 2000).

Ditch That Jerk: Dealing With Men Who Control and Hurt Women. Pamela Jayne (Hunter House, 2000).

Emotionally Involved: The Impact of Researching Rape. Rebecca Campbell (Routledge, 2001).

Getting Free: You Can End Abuse and Take Your Life Back. Ginny Nicarthy (WA: Seal Press, 1997).

The Gift of Fear. Gavin De Becker (Dell, 1998).

Growing Beyond Abuse: A Workbook for Survivors of Sexual Exploitation or Childhood Sexual Abuse. Signe L. Nestingen and Laurel Ruth Lewis (MN: Omni Recovery Inc., 1990).

Growing Beyond Survival: A Self-Help Toolkit for Managing Traumatic Stress. Elizabeth G. Vermilyea (MD: Sidran Press, 2000).

Healing the Trauma of Abuse: A Woman's Workbook. Mary Ellen Copeland and Maxine Harris (CA: New Harbinger Publications, 2000).

The Hired Hand: A Case of Clergy Abuse. Donna E. Scott (America Publishing, 2001).

I Can't Get Over It: A Handbook for Trauma Survivors, 2nd edition. Aphrodite Matsakis (CA: New Harbinger Publications, 1996).

I Never Called It Rape: The Ms. Report on Recognizing, Fighting, and Surviving Date and Acquaintance Rape. Robin Warshaw (NY: Harper Perennial, 1994).

If He is Raped: A Guidebook for Parents, Partners, Spouses, and Friends. Alan McEvoy, Debbie Rollo, and Jeff Brookings (FL: Learning Publications Inc., 2003).

If She Is Raped: A Guidebook for Husbands, Fathers, and Male Friends. Alan W. McEvoy and Jeff B. Brookings (FL: Learning Publications Inc., 1991).

If You Are Raped: What Every Woman Needs to Know. Kathryn
M. Johnson (FL: Learning Publications Inc., 1985).

It Happened to Me: A Teen's Guide to Overcoming Sexual Abuse.
William Lee Carter (CA: New Harbinger Publications, 2002).

Male on Male Rape. Michael Scarce (MA: Perseus Publishing, 1997).

*May I Kiss You? A Candid Look at Dating, Communication, Respect,
& Sexual Assault Awareness.* Mike Domitrz (WI: Awareness
Publications LLC, 2003).

*The Other Side of Silence: Women Tell About Their Experiences
with Date Rape.* Christine Carter (Avocus Publishing, 1995).

Rape in Marriage. Diane E.H. Russell (Indiana University Press, 1990).

Real Rape. Susan Estrich (Harvard University Press, 1988).

Recovering from Rape (2nd edition). Linda Ledray (NY: Henry Holt
and Company, 1994).

Secret Survivors: Uncovering Incest and Its After effects in Women.
Sue E. Blume (Ballantine Books Inc.,1997).

*Sex in the Forbidden Zone: When Men in Power—Therapists,
Doctors, Clergy, Teachers and Others—Betray Women's Trust.*
Peter Rutter (Fawcett Book Group, 1996).

Sexual Assault In Context: Teaching College Men About Gender. Christopher Kilmartin and Alan Berkowitz (FL: Learning Publications, 2000).

Stopping Rape: A Challenge for Men. Rus Ervin Funk (PA: New Society Publishers, 1993).

Strong at the Broken Places: Overcoming the Trauma of Childhood Abuse. Linda Sanford (Avon Books, 1990).

Surviving Childhood Sexual Abuse: Practical Self-Help for Adults Who Were Sexually Abused As Children. Carolyn Ainscough and Kay Toon (Perseus Publishing, 2000).

Surviving the Silence: Black Women's Stories of Rape. Charlotte Pierce-Baker (W.W. Norton & Company, 2000).

Survivors and Partners: Healing the Relationships of Sexual Abuse Survivors. Paul A. Hansen (Heron Hill Publishing Co, 1991).

Transforming a Rape Culture (Reprint Edition). Emilie Buchwald, Pamela R. Fletcher, and Martha Roth (Milkweed Editions, 1995).

Trust After Trauma: A Guide to Relationships for Survivors and Those Who Love Them. Aphrodite Matsakis (CA: New Harbinger Publications, 1998).

The Verbally Abusive Relationship: How to Recognize It and How to Respond. Patrician Evans (MA: Adams Media Corporation, 1996).

Victims No Longer: Men Recovering from Incest and Other Sexual Child Abuse (Reprint Edition). Michael Lew (NY: Harper & Row, 1990).

Who's Afraid of the Dark? A Forum of Truth, Support, and Assurance for Those Affected by Rape. Cynthia Carosella (NY: Harper Perennial, 1995).

You Are Not Alone: Guide for Battered Women. Linda P. Rouse (FL: Learning Publications Inc., 1986).

ABOUT THE EDITOR

Mike Domitrz, nationally renowned expert and critically-acclaimed author, has devoted his life to educating society on healthy dating, communication, respect, consent, and sexual assault awareness.

After experiencing the devastation of his sister being sexually assaulted in 1989, Mike was determined to make a difference. Within two years, he had created and designed his own interactive program, "Can I Kiss You? Dating, Communication, Respect, & Sexual Assault Awareness" (www.canikissyou.com) to educate the public on this important issue. His ability to combine a great sense of humor with hard-hitting emotion has made Mike one of America's most sought-after speakers at schools, college campuses, and community events.

In 2003, Mike wrote the popular book, *May I Kiss You?: A Candid Look at Dating, Communication, Respect, & Sexual Assault Awareness* (www.mayikissyoubook.com). Today, he continues to write and travel the country presenting his popular "Can I Kiss You?" program for audiences of all ages. To bring Mike to speak, call (800) 329-9390 or e-mail info@domitrz.com.

ABOUT THE PUBLISHER

Awareness Publications, LLC is committed to providing thought-provoking books and educational materials that inspire people to make positive changes in their lives and in the lives of others.

We are proud to support Mike Domitrz in his mission to heighten society's awareness of the horror and impact of sexual assault. In 2003, Awareness Publications, LLC published Mr. Domitrz's international selling book, *May I Kiss You?: A Candid Look at Dating, Communication, Respect, & Sexual Assault Awareness,* which is now in its second printing (www.mayikissyoubook.com). Filled with over 20 engaging and thought-provoking exercises, the book has been embraced by both students and parents. Educators and counselors in schools and on college campuses continue to rely on *May I Kiss You?* as a powerful educational resource in the classroom.

Publishing *Voices of Courage: Inspirational Stories from Survivors of Sexual Assault* has been a rewarding and fulfilling experience for everyone at Awareness Publications, LLC. The stories shared by these twelve incredible individuals will provide inspiration for generations of readers.

To learn more about Awareness Publications, LLC visit us online at: www.awarenesspublications.com.

VOICES OF COURAGE

Paperback Book *Voices of Courage* $16.95

Total _____books at $16.95 per book $_____

Audio CD of *Voices of Courage* $24.95

Total _____CDs at $24.95 per CD $_____

Sales Tax *(5.6% for Wisconsin residents only)* $_____

Shipping and Handling within the United States
$4.00 for first item and $2.00 for each additional item $_____

TOTAL AMOUNT ENCLOSED   **$_____**
Checks, Money Orders, or Credit Cards accepted
(No cash please)

Payment type

❑ Check / Money Order made payable to Awareness Publications

❑ Credit Card ❑ Visa ❑ Mastercard ❑ American Express

Credit Card No. _____Exp. Date_____

Name on Card (please print)_____

Signature _____

Credit Card Billing Address _____

City _____ State _____Zip _____

Phone _____

E-mail _____

Photocopy this form and mail or fax it to:
Awareness Publications, LLC
P.O. Box 20906, Greenfield, WI 53220-0906
Fax (414) 329-9830 Phone (800) 329-9390

*If books or CDs are being shipped to a different address, please write that address
on the back of this form or attach a separate sheet of paper.*

Order Online at: *www.voicesofcourage.com*